# MENTORING
# & MANAGING
Students *in the* Academic Library

ALA Editions purchases fund advocacy, awareness, and accreditation programs for library professionals worldwide.

# MENTORING & MANAGING
## Students *in the* Academic Library

### Michelle Reale

An imprint of the American Library Association
Chicago     2013

**Michelle Reale** is the access services and outreach librarian at Landman Library, Arcadia University, located in the suburbs of Philadelphia.

Printed in the United States of America
17 16 15 14 13      5 4 3 2 1

Extensive effort has gone into ensuring the reliability of the information in this book; however, the publisher makes no warranty, express or implied, with respect to the material contained herein.

ISBNs: 978-0-8389-1174-7 (paper); 978-0-8389-9620-1 (PDF). For more information on digital formats, visit the ALA Store at alastore.ala.org and select eEditions.

**Library of Congress Cataloging-in-Publication Data**
Reale, Michelle.
 Mentoring and managing students in the academic library / Michelle Reale.
   pages   cm
 Includes bibliographical references and index.
 ISBN 978-0-8389-1174-7
 1. Student library assistants. 2. Academic libraries—Personnel management.
 I. Title.
 Z682.4.S89R43 2012
 023'.3—dc23

2012027377

Cover design by Adrianna Sutton. Cover image © Yuri Arcurs/Shutterstock, Inc.
Composition by Casey Bayer in Andada and Aller.

♾ This paper meets the requirements of ANSI/NISO Z39.48-1992 (Permanence of Paper).

*Dedicated to my parents, Russell and Dorothy Messina, by far my first and best mentors*

*To Dr. Jeanne Buckley with immense gratitude for consistently and gently showing me the way*

*To Mary Gillis and Francine Sabino for such fine attention to detail*

*To Erin Bruno for summing it up in a way that only she could*

# Contents

# Introduction

THE ACTUAL ORIGIN of mentoring as a practice has roots in Greek mythology. When Odysseus left to fight in the Trojan War, he placed his son Telemachus in the care of his most trusted friend, Mentor. In young adulthood, the goddess Athena assumed Mentor's identity as Telemachus went in search of his father. What began as a seemingly masculine tradition now knows no gender limits, though some of the literature would suggest that men prefer to be mentored by men and women by women.

Now, mentoring is a common and increasingly growing practice in nearly every profession, though the concept of mentoring will mean different things to different people in different contexts. At its very basic definition, mentoring is a close relationship between, let us say for clarity's sake, someone who seeks guidance and one who is in the position, by intellect, temperament, and experience, to be able to provide it.

## A Personal Approach

The idea of writing this book came out of the many experiences I have had over the past seven years working closely with students at the suburban university where I am a faculty librarian. Because our library employs so many federally funded work-study students in order to run smoothly and offer the liberal open hours that the campus community enjoys, it is in our interest to hire the best students that we can, train them well, and teach them something along the way about how to "be" in the work world, while also encouraging their own career goals whatever they may be.

While all of this seems such an obvious approach—indeed, isn't all of the above what we should be doing, anyway?—the day-to-day responsibilities of most librarians in the university setting do not allow for the time it will often take to really work with a student who may be shy, reluctant, bored, or simply uninterested in the job at hand. Not every student who gets placed at the library wants to be there. In fact, with a few very strong exceptions, most of the students who may approach you at the beginning of any given semester, their work placement in hand, probably did not want to work in the library; it was simply the luck of the draw. Stereotypes being what they are (i.e., fierce and persistent), to many students, especially those fresh from high school, the atmosphere of a library is believed to be one of stagnant, mind-numbing boredom, to say nothing of the negative image held firmly in their minds of the librarians who work there.

As for the librarian's point of view, the time it takes to train a student in all of the various aspects of technology and customer service will send up a collective sigh among most of us in the profession. It is a difficult task, at best, to give consistent and even service with a group of students for whom work is not their first priority. We understand this, though, at the outset, and work toward our goals anyway. Our students are extremely valuable commodities in our libraries, a great boon to the functioning of the day-to-day operation, and necessary to keep the library open when most, if not all, professional staff have left for the day.

For both librarians and students, there seems to be so much to overcome, but I suppose that is why they call it "work." Working with students in the library setting is just that: work. And the hard work is, indeed, the very beginning of the mentoring process whether or not you frame it that way in your own mind. Working with students is different from working with your colleagues. Obvious reasons aside, our students are a work in progress; they are in formation. We have the capacity to inspire and influence them in incredibly positive ways.

For some students (not all, of course), the library job may be their first job ever. One of the most basic responsibilities we have, then, is to tell them what is expected and then show them how to "be" in the workplace by modeling behavior. My idea of what we do with our students in the library came about, quite honestly, from a sense of deep frustration early on when I tended to perceive certain students as being deliberately uncommunicative, lazy, or unwilling to learn, when really they were simply shy, did not know, fully, what they were expected to do, and did not know how to take the first step. I learned quickly that their library job will probably be their "kindest" job ever and that I was perfectly positioned to teach them professional behavior, instill confidence, give them projects that will not only help me and the library in general but give them a sense of how their part, small as it might be, is part of the greater whole—and, hopefully, of the greater good!

This is most assuredly a process that takes time and careful attention. For me, personally, it has meant taking a more holistic approach to my students in order to see them, really see them, as people in their own right, with their own fears, feelings, responsibilities (quite apart, of course, from their library job), relationships, strengths, and shortcomings. They do not come to me "perfect," which is a good thing since I myself am not either. Remembering that we were once as they were will help to frame their experience and leave both student and librarian open to all of the possibilities for learning.

## The Reality

I would be remiss if I did not mention that it is not easy. And that you cannot mentor everyone at the same level. And that some will reject you outright. And some may eventually turn on you, suddenly rejecting everything you have tried to do, leaving you lost and disappointed. But that's okay, because a mentoring relationship is not unlike other relationships we must negotiate every day with others in our lives: they take constant work. Sometimes we are successful. Sometimes we aren't. But in the library we are perfectly positioned among and within the educational environment to offer so much to the students we are incredibly lucky to have.

I have experienced nearly every possible scenario while working toward mentoring students. I have been pleased, ecstatic (especially about those who decide to enter the profession!), disappointed, tired, unsure, and, yes, heartbroken when a mentoring relationship has gone awry. Thankfully, that has happened only once, and in a later chapter I will talk about what to do if that happens.

## The Scope of This Book

This book is not meant to be an exhaustive look at mentoring as a practice in its most formal aspects or in areas outside of the academic library setting, such as in the business, education, or medical fields. Instead, this book will highlight a practical approach to meeting students *where they are* and helping them to work toward greater confidence in themselves as people and to achieve particular goals while learning to be capable participants in the workplace. There is precious little information about the actual act of mentoring students who work in academic libraries, so much of the information contained in this book is based on general aspects of mentoring and adapted for the librarian's use. Much of the book blends the general tenets of mentoring with my own experience with students whom I employ.

Throughout this book, you will find sections highlighting various aspects of mentoring students in the library, both philosophic and practical, two aspects that cannot be separated from each other. Paying close attention to some practical aspects, such as hiring, I have found, minimizes a multitude of problems later on, though it does not mitigate them entirely. And while I have said that a student may come to you unwilling and with preconceived notions about working in the library, it is up to you as the student's potential supervisor whether that particular student is one whom you choose to hire. For instance, I, personally, would not have the time or stamina to work with and mentor all fifty of the work-study students I have each semester if they did not want to work in the library, so a short but careful interview is incredibly helpful. Still, as a librarian, you will find that you will be teaching all of your students how to work and mentoring a portion of them in one way or another. There should be no guilt in being unable to mentor each and every student who comes your way. It is, simply put, not possible. When you begin the process of thinking about mentoring, *however informal you will find the process,* it will become immediately apparent to you that it is a personal investment in time, emotions, and other resources.

What you will find in this book will be, I think, helpful no matter what the size of your library or the number of students you employ. Be advised that mentoring, no matter how informal the process, is like any relationship: personal and unique. And relationships tend to unfold in their own time. As always, guidelines are meant to be just that: guidelines, not hard-and-fast prescriptives for everyone in every situation.

Far from being the stern, wrinkly-lipped, "shushing" people dressed in droll colors, trolling the stacks for transgressors, librarians are highly educated professionals who will "meet" the student in a variety of places, for example, as a teacher in the classroom, as a supervisor in the library, and as a research guide at the reference desk. We are perfectly positioned to make a difference in the lives of students. If most students can remember a teacher or librarian who made their life miserable, imagine the effect of one who has done just the opposite. In the library world, that has the potential to be downright revolutionary.

*Merriam-Webster* defines the word *mentor* simply—"a trusted guide or counselor"—and classifies it as both a noun and a verb. As librarians working closely with students every day but never thinking of what we do as mentoring, we need to rethink our role with the students who work with us. Every one of us, at the very least, has the potential to be a trusted guide. At our very best, we can be wise counselors, attentive to the development of the students as future professionals (in any career they may choose) as well as training them to be an asset to our library. As professionals, we will have a myriad of situations in which to offer students not just mentoring "moments," but days, weeks, months, and years. Investing time in our students now means that all of us, in one way or another, reap the benefits later on as our students leave the confines of the educational institute in which they have been safely ensconced and go out into the world to be the people they were meant to be: confident and capable.

# 1

# Mentoring Students in the Library Setting

*What we must decide is perhaps how we are valuable, rather than how valuable we are.*
—F. Scott Fitzgerald

MOST ACADEMIC LIBRARIES could not function or provide extended hours without the help of work-study students. Federally funded work-study students are the backbone of most if not all college libraries. Often, they are the public face of the library, indeed, the first impression that visitors—faculty members, trustees, alums, students or prospective students—will see upon entering.

It is clearly in the best interest of libraries to train their students well, not only in the art of service (which I truly believe is an art), but as young adults who will be entering and facing the actual work world themselves. In other words, a library job can be just another job (and most will certainly see it that way) and the student standing before you can be just one of many going through the motions of showing up when they are told to, if you are willing to forego the larger possibility of being a mentor. That is, if you are content to remain in a silo, small and safe, where you tend to your professional duties, divorced from the very students you serve both in the library and the university at large.

Mentoring students in the academic library has larger implications. We, as library professionals, are at the same time partnering with the educational process. And if we aren't, we should be. This larger relationship is a responsibility worth taking on and holds rewards for both the librarian and the student mentee. For the librarian, the opportunity

- to make a positive difference;
- to teach professional behavior in a professional setting; and
- to help student retention

can be personally fulfilling. For the student,

- gaining a realistic view of expectations in the workplace;
- building student confidence;
- having the opportunity to learn, grow, and excel under guidance;
- gaining valuable skills for a résumé; and
- providing the capacity for the mentoring relationship to continue beyond the library job

are clearly rewarding experiences. For both parties the capacity for the mentoring relationship to continue beyond the job is a bonus, as well.

Marina Snow, a librarian at California State University, details in a fine essay, "Librarian as Mentor," the many benefits a student gains by choosing, by happenstance, a librarian as an informal mentor. The reasons she states make perfect sense: librarians are more largely available than most professors, who have limited office hours. A reference desk is usually staffed for most of the day and part of the evening in most institutions, increasing the incidence and serendipity of the "drop by." Younger students may view the librarian as a survivor of academe, while older students enjoy the opportunity to share common work experiences, values, and challenges.

Snow goes on to make a point that I believe in very strongly: that the conversation and practice of mentoring students in the library is not to advocate a formal program to be instituted by "already overburdened reference librarians," but that close and concerned relationships between librarians and students can be both beneficial and rewarding to everyone involved. She goes on to state how often these relationships live beyond the college experience, which gives credence to both the necessity and the value of the practice. If students can gain benefit from such an informal mentoring transaction as the one that Snow discusses, then how much more of an impact might a more deliberate mentoring relationship have in the academic library and in the life of the student?[1]

While mentoring means different things to different people in different situations in the context of the academic library, it will often take on a less formal aspect in practice. For the purposes presented here, mentoring can be any process by which a student is taught or nurtured along in professionalism as it relates immediately to his or her job setting and to the work world at large. In addition, the mentor acts as a kind and concerned friend, who encourages and believes in his or her students' efforts toward their career goals. We engage in all these processes in the setting in which we will encounter these students: in the library.

How this is approached and accomplished will be unique depending upon the personality of the professional, the student, and any number of other factors. It can be a more formal or informal process: it can occur daily or weekly or monthly, in person, on the phone, or online. However and how often the practice occurs, its existence is most important to the development of the student and such efforts should not be diminished.

There are those who might argue that mentoring is a specific activity whose function is tightly focused on specific career goals and whose place among student workers in an academic library is misplaced. After all, the students are working their campus jobs usually for one reason and one reason only: to earn money. How many of them are actually working in the library because their lifelong dream is to become an academic librarian? Many students, at least at my institution, have no idea whatsoever what librarians do all day. Even the fact that librarians need master's degrees, more often than not, will befuddle students: "A master's degree—for what?" they ask. How many do we imagine actually want to go into the field? When we employ students, we must recognize that their main goals (to receive an education, to make money) are not mutually exclusive of the goals of mentoring students in the academic library.

There is much wisdom in being able to simply "meet students where they are." That means to be able to accept them, initially as we find them, and make an honest attempt to discern what their goals are. If we, as academic librarians and other paraprofessionals, are working side by side with students day in and day out, we have to seize the opportunity to help them along in their job, which will most likely be the kindest they will ever encounter. It is a great opportunity for both the librarian and the student. The payoffs are numerous and myriad and not just for the student. And what would be so terrible if a few who were helped along the way actually became interested in the changing field of library science?

Carl Jung coined the term "The Dream" to describe career and lifestyle aspirations held in early adulthood. Every student we encounter in the library setting has unique aspirations and dreams, though some students may not exactly be aware of what they are. Developing life goals is a process and unfolds over a period of time. In fact, we may encounter students who, during the entire time that we know them during their college years, will not be able to figure out what it is, exactly, that they want to do with their lives. A few will be so inner-directed that any sort of mentoring relationship attempted may be viewed by them as simply icing on the cake, making it easy for us. For those who have dreams and goals, but no clear blueprint for how to get there, and no one to whom they can address the "Big Questions," mentoring provides a safe and solid road map that can get them, if not from point A to point B, then at least from A.1 to A.2.

Developmental processes cannot and should not be rushed. Development may not be linear. Just as we think a student may have leaped a few steps ahead, he takes two steps back. Though it often takes a great deal of patience for the mentor to watch and wait, that is part and parcel of the job.

The best kind of mentoring is focused on the student's needs and expectations and not on a rigid agenda that the librarian may have in mind. This should not be confused with asking and expecting students to perform their job requirements to satisfaction and hopefully beyond. It means, though, that the results of the "extra added value" you give as a mentor with careful attention, guidance, and structure will often occur over an extended period of time and cannot be rushed. Developmental processes must be honored and a trusting relationship must be given the time that it needs to grow and develop. The amount of time will likely be different with each student. Mentoring that occurs in the academic library setting sets the tone for collegiality both on the job and during the college experience at large.

## NOTE

1. Marina Snow, "Librarian as Mentor," *Journal of Academic Librarianship* 16 (July 1990).

## RESOURCES

Awaya, Allen, Hunter McEwan, Deborah Heyler, Sandy Linsky, Donna Lum, and Pamela Wakukawa. "Mentoring as a Journey." *Teaching and Teacher Education* 19 (2003): 43–56.

Baker, Vicki L., and Kimberly A. Griffin. "Beyond Mentoring and Advising: Toward Understanding the Role of Faculty 'Developers' in Student Success." *About Campus* 14, no. 6 (2010): 2–8.

Baldwin, David A. *Supervising Student Employees in Academic Libraries.* Englewood, NJ: Libraries Unlimited, 1991.

Jacobi, Maryann. "Mentoring and Undergraduate Academic Success: A Literature Review." *Review of Educational Research* 61, no. 4 (1991): 505–32.

Lantos, Geoffrey P. "Nurturing Professionalism in Our Students." *Marketing Educator* 18, no. 2 (1999). http://faculty.stonehill.edu/glantos/Lantos1/PDF_Folder/Pub_arts_pdf/ Professionalism.pdf.

Monaghan, J. "Mentoring: Person, Process, Practice and Problems." *British Journal of Educational Studies* 40, no. 3 (1992): 248–63.

Speizer, Jeanne J. "Role Models, Mentors, and Sponsors: The Elusive Concepts." *Signs* 6, no. 4 (1981): 692–712.

Zey, Michael G. "A Mentor for All Reasons." *Personnel Journal* 67, no. 1 (1988): 46–51.

# Hiring Students

## Not Business as Usual

*Selecting the right person for the right job is the largest part of coaching.*
—Phillip Crosby

THERE IS A misconception in academic libraries that we must hire any student who is assigned to us or who asks for a job. While I am not advocating the (bad) practice of turning anyone away, I am an advocate of the interview process, as I mentioned in chapter 1. While it seems a bit overreaching to require students to have a résumé (unless the job requires a very special skill), mainly because they will probably not have any related experience (though they might), the interview process is vital to ascertaining whether the student possesses a desire to do the job.

Interviewing the student is the best way not only to obtain firsthand information about students, such as their majors, their hometowns, their interests, and their extracurricular activities, but also to give them enough information about the job to help them to decide if the library in fact is the place they want to be. A semester can be agonizingly long for anyone supervising or mentoring a recalcitrant student, and the interview process helps to correct misconceptions. Many students who will be assigned to the library may have preconceived notions about the library: that it is an uninteresting and boring place where they go to suffer!

# Types

If you have had the opportunity to hire students in your library, you can see attitude types emerge over time. I have made a list of the types I have seen over the years, which has helped me to assess my approach to each type of student behavior.

This list is not used as a categorization as such—labels are rarely helpful. Rather, these categories help me to assess a student's work style, allowing me to proceed accordingly.

### The Go Get 'Ems

Students presenting this style want to make a good impression. They like to shine. They are gregarious, they will shake your hand, and they will often regale you with stories of their dependability and many accomplishments. They do, indeed, make a great impression. They do, however, fizzle out fast when they realize that much of the work is "teamwork" and they become one among many.

### The Overconfident

Students presenting this style will often express surprise at this thing called the librarian profession: "You mean you need a degree to do this job?" Often they will correct you, question why things are done a certain way (which in and of itself is not a bad thing), and give you pointed suggestions on how they can make things better.

### The Too Cool for School

These students will feel as though they should not be held to the same standards as others. There will be certain jobs they may deem "menial" (filling photocopiers with paper, shelf reading, discarding old books), that are beneath them and not really "teaching" (read benefiting) them in any way.

### The Disinterested

This type may have come to the library for a variety of reasons: a work-study assignment, a misconception that the job would allow time to get schoolwork done, and so on. Whatever the case may be, the student, for one reason or another, is simply not interested in the work at hand.

### The Helpful

This student tends to be quiet, but helpful. I treasure students who eagerly accept tasks as they are given. I have often found that the helpful type also makes incredibly wonderful suggestions about how to do things and, in general, will often create shortcuts to procedures, organize work spaces, and engage well with others. The librarian, though, can make the mistake of becoming too dependent on students who are helpful—because they are usually quite capable as well!

These are only a few types that I have encountered. There are many others. This list may or may not be a true representation of the students you will encounter in your own library, but some may seem familiar. Be cautious of your first impressions of a student—both good impressions and bad ones. I have encountered any number of students who have come to me bright and shiny and then have gone on to disappoint early and often. Some students about whom I had serious doubts grew into the job beautifully and developed pride in what they were doing and a newfound interest in a profession they previously knew nothing about. I have noticed that, in general, the slower the starter, the better the worker. These students build skills and learn professionalism over time. Those who come on strong leave (or are asked to leave) in the same way (often with attendant drama), which is a draining experience for everyone involved.

It is always a good idea to explain to a student at the interview stage that employment is "conditional" upon a number of factors, including punctuality, ability, customer service, and other aspects of the job. A colleague of mine pointed out that "conditional" could and in fact should go both ways between the librarian and the student. Let students know that if the job does not work out for them (for any reason) they, too, are free to give notice at the end of the trial period. This provides a graceful escape route for a student who, though well-meaning, does not want to remain in the job. I once had a student who I was extremely fond of and who I considered an excellent worker. She began to miss shifts here and there and began being lackadaisical on the job, behavior I had not seen from her at all before. When I let her go, with many misgivings, and quite frankly with great disappointment, she breathed a sigh of relief. She'd really been interested in certain aspects of community service and wanted a job that allowed her to work with different organizations on campus. She didn't want to quit and unbelievably preferred to be fired!

## Making It Official

Students should fill out paperwork before they begin to work. At the very least, you should have their contact information. I usually give my students five forms that they must carefully read and initial before they begin working:

1. Job Description (fig. 2.1)
2. Contact Information Sheet/Commitment to Making a Difference (fig. 2.2)
3. Circulation Desk Rules for Student Workers (fig. 2.3)
4. Grounds for Dismissal (fig. 2.4)
5. Pennsylvania Library Association Statement on Libraries, Privacy, and the USA PATRIOT Act (fig. 2.5)

The paperwork process itself lends a bit of gravitas when we hire students, causing them to realize that there is more to working in the library than someone just giving the go-ahead and then one day they show up. It is good for students to understand that there are procedures in place. Moreover, having them read and sign the forms in your presence ensures that they have read and presumably understand what you have put forth. Giving them time to ask questions is a good idea and will help to dispel notions up front. For some students this will be the first time that they have had a job. What they know of working could be what they have overhead from their parents in their own homes. I once had a student who signed up for circulation desk hours three days a week that bridged the usual lunch times—from noon to 2 p.m. She asked me if she would be able to take a half-hour lunch from 12:30 to 1 p.m. I told her why that wasn't appropriate. When I relayed that story to some library friends of mine, they laughed. But really, how was she to know? Now, however, that is information that I always mention up front.

## The Check-In

Early in the trial period would be a good time to ask the student, "How are we doing here?" This gives the student the opportunity to discuss his or her thoughts about the job, which will open the door to any feedback you'd like to give at this time. This won't mitigate the future occurrence of any problems or issues but plants the seeds of a working, mentoring relationship.

Follow-up check-ins with new students should occur frequently. Because it is conceivable (and perhaps probable) that you will hire students for shifts

## Position:

Circulation Desk Worker

## Description:

The circulation desk worker is the face of Landman Library, as s/he is the person patrons interact with most often. A circulation desk worker is responsible for manning the desk, shelving books, answering nonreference questions about the library, such as "Where can I find_____?" and "What are the library hours today?," and keeping the library's books and media in order. Circulation desk workers are also responsible for helping patrons in need of assistance, such as those who cannot find a book or who are having trouble with computers/printers. A circulation desk worker should be prompt and energetic, accommodating to those in need, and able to complete tasks in an orderly fashion. Knowledge of the Library of Congress System of Classification is not required to obtain the position; however, it is imperative that this skill is learned on the job.

## Report to:

Michelle Reale

Ex: 2139

realem@arcadia.edu

If you have any questions, do not hesitate to ask a fellow worker or staff member.

**Fig. 2.1** Job Description

that you yourself will never work, finding a way to mentor them from afar is essential. Checking in with student (or other) supervisors who are working with them on their shifts, to help assess their strengths and weaknesses, should be part of this effort. Providing feedback is important for the student, though do not expect this step to mitigate all problems. It is just a step in the process. One of many.

While the aim is to have happy, reliable students we can help during their college tenure, realistically this will not always be possible. This doesn't mean we shouldn't try. Students who do work in the library and are satisfied doing so are likely to be good ambassadors of the library in general and provide

# Arcadia University Landman Library

Name _____ Semester/Year _____

Hourly Rate _____ Check One:  ☐ Freshman  ☐ Sophomore  ☐ Junior  ☐ Senior

Local Address (Dorm + Room if Resident) _____

_____

Campus Phone _____ Cell Phone _____

Home Phone _____ E-mail Address_____

Permanent Address _____

_____

## MY COMMITMENT TO MAKING A DIFFERENCE

I have read the Landman Library Student Manual and understand what is expected of me in terms of my behavior and responsibilities while at work. I understand that I am an essential member of the library staff and serve an important role in the day-to-day operations of the library as it serves both the college community and members of the general public. I agree to adhere to the policies stated in the manual.

I agree to work at the Landman Library for the hours scheduled. Also, I agree to reschedule for the extended hours for exams in order to provide needed coverage at the library. If I am not able to work my scheduled hours, it is my responsibility to find a substitute from the list provided by the library and to notify the Circulation Desk Supervisor.

I have read the above and agree to work at the Landman Library. I am interested in MAKING A DIFFERENCE!

Signature _____ Date_____

**Fig. 2.2**   Contact Information Sheet/Commitment to Making a Difference

## Landman Library, Arcadia University
## Circulation Desk Rules

- Show up for your shift on time and ready to work. Do not schedule appointments during your work hours.
- Find a replacement from the list of circulation desk workers if you must miss a shift. E-mail Michelle or your night supervisor.
- If you don't know, ask! Not knowing is not an excuse.
- Mute cell phones while working.
- If all assigned duties are completed and the desk is quiet, you may have the opportunity to do your homework. However, please do not come to work expecting to be able to study for a test, complete a paper, etc.
- Do not send visitors directly back to anyone's office or desk area. Inform staff members that someone wishes to see them up front.
- Please be proactive with your job. Upon coming on to your shift, consult the list of duties to be completed and contribute.
- Please act professionally while on your shift.
- Patron confidentiality is of the utmost importance.
- Never leave the circulation desk unattended.
- Make sure that the next shift has arrived before you leave.
- Respect library staff and their work areas.
- Enter your shift hours after you have worked them.
- Take pride in what you do and realize that you are the public "face" of the library.

**Fig. 2.3** Circulation Desk Rules for Student Workers

excellent library services in particular. Unfortunately, the opposite is true of those who do not enjoy or who do not prove successful in their library jobs.

Hiring students and letting them go are often fine lines to tread. The process of recruitment, interviewing, creating expectations, and setting realistic goals concerning work assignments will help to make things run as smoothly as possible. Those students who understand the steps and let themselves be guided and, dare I say, *nurtured* along through the process are not only keepers, but in all likelihood will be the ones you will retain for the length of their college years, thus allowing a mentoring relationship to develop naturally over time.

## Grounds For Dismissal

It is MY responsibility to talk to my supervisor, Michelle Reale, ASAP if there is ANY problem that is impacting my performance or attendance.

Circ Desk: 215-572-2975

Michelle Reale: 215-572-2139 (Office)

**ALL EMPLOYMENT IS CONDITIONAL** dependent upon satisfactory completion of a four-week trial period.

You may be dismissed for the following reasons:

- Excessive lateness
- Missing shifts without notifying Michelle or your Night Supervisor
- Consistent unsatisfactory job performance
- Incorrectly reporting hours in the time sheet system
- Unauthorized use of library facilities, materials, and/or supplies
- Refusal to do assigned tasks or doing them reluctantly or without attention to detail
- Disrespect toward staff, students, or anyone else while you are working
- Showing up for work under the influence of alcohol or any illegal substances
- Blatant disrespect to your supervisor, coworkers, library staff, or others
- Dressing inappropriately or using inappropriate language

I HAVE READ THE ABOVE AND UNDERSTAND THE GROUNDS FOR DISMISSAL.

Student Signature _____ Date_____

**Fig. 2.4**   Grounds for Dismissal

Pennsylvania Library Association (PLA)
STATEMENT ON LIBRARIES, PRIVACY, AND THE USA PATRIOT ACT
Adopted April 7, 2004

Patron Privacy is a fundamental component of free and open access to information. The confidentiality of library records is protected under Pennsylvania law (24 P.S. Section 428): "Records related to circulation of library materials which contain the name or other personally identifying details shall be confidential and shall not be made available to anyone except by a court order in a criminal proceeding."

**Fig. 2.5** Pennsylvania Library Association Statement on Libraries, Privacy, and the USA PATRIOT Act

# Strategies

## Remember the Interviewing Process

This is a step that many librarians, mistakenly, seem to feel is unnecessary, believing that they have no choice in their student workers. On the contrary, it is vitally important that librarians utilize the ability to choose who will be working side by side, and, to a great extent, who will be representing the staff at the first desk that anyone sees, the circulation desk, upon entering the library.

## Provide a Written Job Description

Students need to understand the demands and scope of the job they are applying for or have been assigned to. Not one among us could reasonably expect to do well in a job without first knowing all that it entails. Go over the job description with the students during the interview so that if they should have questions you will be able to answer them right away.

## Match, as Much as Possible, Interests and Skills

Placing a painfully shy student at the circulation desk will not help the student or set the stage for good customer service. Likewise, an outgoing, service-oriented student buried in the archives is a waste of talent.

## Try to Avoid Making Student Employment Decisions on the Spot

It is a good idea to "sleep on it" for a number of reasons, although desperation or need sometimes demands otherwise. Sometimes first impressions are, indeed, the best impressions. But sometimes they are not. Moreover, waiting before you hire gives the student the (correct) impression that placing the right person in the right job is worthy of careful consideration and mimics the actual process in the "real world."

## Make Expectations Clear

The student should have a mutually agreed-upon schedule and know the procedure for calling out sick or finding replacements for her shift should the occasion arise. And it will.

## Keep a Paper Trail

A file should be kept on each student containing, at the very least, the student's contact information. Other pertinent information, such as signed confidentiality forms and a signed job description, will also go in this file.

## Institute a Trial Period

This is an important aspect of hiring and working with students and it would be impossible to put too fine a point on this. A fair trial period, in most but not all instances, would be four weeks. A student should not take a job for granted and should be forewarned that if expectations have not been met within the trial period, perhaps the work-study placement is not a good fit. At this time the librarian will have to decide whether to continue working with the student or if the student would be better served by seeking employment elsewhere.

## Train the Student for the Job

I would speculate that most instances of miscommunication on the job are due to lack of training. Students want to do well and want to be perceived as capable, but if we do not provide them with training, we put them in the unfair position of failing. Lack of training is a failure on our part, not theirs. Ideally, training should be both an early employment experience and an ongoing opportunity, and it should be consistently available across departments.

## Make It Clear How to Communicate Problems or Difficulties

When I first began supervising students at the circulation desk, I made a glaring error in not communicating the proper "chain of command" for communicating difficulties or concerns. I found my students were going to various colleagues in an effort to deal with situations that were in my domain. I always encourage my students to consult with my colleagues, but I needed to more clearly explain to them that in matters of circulation, I was the person to whom they should speak. Students soon understood that in my absence it was perfectly acceptable to have another staff member or professional help them out with whatever was needed.

### Make It Clear Whom They Work For

Well-meaning colleagues may see your students sitting at the circulation desk and assign them various duties to save themselves time. My reason for opposing this is that it confuses the student as to whom he takes his orders from and has the potential to make the student feel exploited. Students tend to work best when their jobs are communicated to them through one person—the person who hired them.

One day there were two students at the circulation desk and a full cart of books to be shelved. I had asked my students to get started on putting the books away. I went back to my office and began to work when I realized the circulation desk phone kept ringing. I picked up the line, took care of the question, and walked out to the circulation desk and no one was there. I asked one of my colleagues if she had seen any of my students. She told me that she had one making copies for her. Ah! When the student came back I told her that if she wants to do a task for anyone besides me, she should ask me first and, as well, make sure that the front desk is always covered. She apologized profusely and explained that since another librarian had asked her to do something, she thought that it would be okay. I understood perfectly that to the student this would seem reasonable. Now, when I train students, I make this clear. And I have, as well, told my colleagues that it works better if they ask me first if they'd like one of my students to do something for me.

# Conclusion

As much as is reasonably possible, the procedure for hiring students should mimic the one that students will encounter when looking for a job in the future. Taking them through the steps is an important skill we can teach them as it prepares them for the inevitable. Giving them the time to understand the position and the rules and expectations that go with it gives them a fair start.

There will often be the temptation to just let a student begin and "learn on the job," but not only is that not fair to the student, which can make her feel nervous and suffer a lack of confidence, but it always seems to backfire: in the effort to save time, the librarian will eventually and undoubtedly be put in the position of both training and undoing bad work habits that may already have been applied by the student. Applying good hiring practices goes a long way in gaining valuable student help in the library as well as helping to position our students for present and future success.

## RESOURCES

Darwin, Ann. "Critical Reflections on Mentoring in Work Settings." *Adult Education Quarterly* 50, no. 3 (May 2000): 197–211.

Katham, Jane M., and Michael D. Kathman. "Training Student Employees for Quality Service." *Journal of Academic Librarianship* 26, no. 3 (2000): 176–82.

Kenney, Donald J., and Frances O. Painter. "Recruiting, Hiring and Assessing Student Workers in Academic Libraries." *Journal of Library Administration* 21, no. 3/4 (1995): 29–45.

Slagell, Jeff, and Jeanne M. Langendorfer. "Don't Tread on Me: The Art of Supervising Student Assistants." *Serials Librarian* 44, no. 3/4 (2003): 279–84.

# The Nuts and Bolts of Hiring and Training Students

*Tell me and I'll forget; show me and I may remember; involve me and I'll understand.*
—Chinese proverb

*Excellence is an art won by training and habituation. We do not act rightly because we have virtue or excellence, but we rather have those because we have acted rightly. We are what we repeatedly do. Excellence, then, is not an act but a habit.*
—Aristotle

IT IS A good idea for every library to put into place both a philosophy and a set of practices for hiring, training, and working with students. This will usually be a blend between the strictures of what is required by federal and state law as well as what is fair to the student and what makes sense for your particular library and your particular institution. Often the best opportunities for mentoring happen when your students are well placed within your department. The nuts and bolts of student employment will vary from institution to institution, and the procedures and policies may differ. What I offer you here is an explanation of Federal and Nonfederal Work-Study. As a supervisor, familiarizing yourself with these procedures ensures that there is no interruption in student employment.

## Hiring Students for the Library

Students often want to work in the library because they perceive it as an easy job: short on pressure and demands, long on time to study and chitchat with friends over the circulation desk. Students who seek employment at the library should be disabused of such notions, if indeed they have them, right away. Students inquiring about a job at the library should be handed a description of available jobs within the library. It helps to have these job descriptions written by the staff in their individual departments and to see to it that they are updated each semester as duties and responsibilities are added or taken away. This job description should include any special skills the student may need to possess. When a student fails at a job, it can often be because the student was not well suited to it to begin with.

Matching the right student to the right job is an important aspect of the hiring process and decreases the amount of negative interactions that may result when a student, whether real or perceived, does not feel equal to the task. A campus job for a student is an important part of the college experience, but only a *part* of that experience. Managing expectations here is important, too; otherwise we are setting the student up to fail by expecting more than the student can reasonably be expected to give. We should bear in mind, too, that the student's studies will (and always should) come first.

- Provide the student with a job description. (See fig. 2.1 in chapter 2.)
- Have student fill out the proper paperwork in the form of a basic application or contact information sheet.
- Interview the student for suitability in temperament and ability.
- Set a time period as a "trial" for both the student and yourself and reevaluate the student's performance and comfort level in the job at the end of that time period. Three weeks to one month into the job seems to be an appropriate time period during a semester.
- Explain expectations clearly.
- Create a schedule that works for the student.
- Communicate information about the library by introducing the student to your colleagues and coworkers.
- Provide the student with an organizational chart so that she can contextualize her own valuable contribution to the functioning of one of the most important academic organizations on campus.
- Explain library policies.
- Communicate the rationales for procedures.
- Model patience and professionalism.
- Help the student to master one skill before moving on to another.

It helps to evaluate the time you feel that you will need to train a student. This will help you to decide whether you will be able to take on students who may not possess all of the skills and qualifications ideally required for the job. Training is often an intense and time-consuming endeavor. From a student point of view, most student library jobs will look deceptively simple. For instance, while the circulation desk may look pretty straightforward to a student when he comes in to return books or to check them out, he may be surprised to find out that there are an endless number of details a student worker must keep track of, including all of the different rules for various users (e.g., faculty, community, alumni), terms of academic reserves, library policies, and so on. Once a student is trained in the basics it is often helpful (and wise) to have other students help the new student out by answering questions and helping to smooth the transition.

Often a student will desire a job in the library but will not be the best "fit." Students often perceive a library job as an "easy" job, a place where only a "warm body" is needed and where they can get a maximum amount of homework done. As I have said earlier, this attitude will usually present itself fairly quickly, making good and thorough training that much more important. Hiring students without giving them the amount of time and instruction needed to succeed is both unfair to the students and counterproductive to getting the job done.

And what about students with résumés? I love them! I once had a first-year student present me with one, which naturally surprised me. The seriousness and effort with which this student approached her search for a job was quite impressive, to say the least. The intention to prepare and present me with a résumé is, in all honesty, much more important to me than what is actually on it, although I am always happy to see some kind of experience—in anything! Bagging groceries, washing cars, and even babysitting, to give just a few examples, all exemplify a level of work/job experience and commitment. One of the wonderful things about on-campus jobs is that most of them will presume no level of expertise, save for the willingness to work and reliability. With training, practice, and the proper support, students will achieve confidence and skill that will, in turn, make them eligible for rehiring. Students who are well trained in their campus job usually turn out to be wonderful peer trainers to others, as well.

## A Student's First Shift

Orientation is just that—orienting a student as a new worker—and it is important. This contextualizing is a step that cannot be skipped. A student will know the library from a totally different viewpoint as a student, or perhaps she (unfortunately) will not know it at all. In either case, she must be shown her new environment from a service-oriented point of view.

I like to make my students feel welcome by introducing them to everyone from the library director to the administrative assistant and all those in between. I make it clear what appropriate behavior is in the workplace. I get into the particulars about where they can store their lunch, hang their coat, place their backpack, where the restroom is, and where they can heat their soup! The simplest tasks come first. At the circulation desk, I emphasize phone etiquette, checking books in, checking books out, learning the Library of Congress classification system, and putting books in classification order on a book cart. In subsequent shifts I train them in academic reserves, shelving books, shelf reading, and other points of customer service.

Colleagues are so important not only in helping to keep students on task but also in modeling professional behavior. While it is confusing and less than desirable to have too many people correcting or giving orders to students, I count on my colleagues to point out and correct student mistakes that need immediate attention. In every case my colleagues have done this in the most respectful and least intrusive way, in order to *teach* the student the way something should be done, instead of being punitive.

## Forms

Students should fill out new intake forms in your department as well as in the department on campus that processes their applications, and so on. These intake forms will vary in different institutions and can be as simple as a contact information sheet, or an actual application. (See the forms in chapter 2.)

I keep duplicate copies of all forms that my students fill out along with any notes about missing shifts, difficulties they may be experiencing with their studies, special initiatives they have been taking, or anything else that might help me to help them on the job or understand "where they are at" if they seem to be having difficulties. It should be noted that this is not a dossier and I have no interest, nor do I think it appropriate, to keep copious notes on various aspects of a student. For me, these notes have come in handy when it was time (and the time always comes) to write the many recommendation letters I am asked to do. It helps, too, when I need to give them feedback, which is a very important part of their job experience.

## Federal Work-Study

While every university will implement and maintain different hiring procedures, most, if not all, will be hiring students who have a Federal Work-Study allotment, part of their financial aid package that will allow them to work a campus job and earn money for either their living expenses or their tuition. Federal Work-Study is a different form of financial aid to students who have demonstrated, through eligibility requirements, financial need. These students will have completed the FAFSA (Free Application for Federal Student Aid) form. This is a form that must be completed each year. Students must be sure to mark "yes" to the question on the form that asks if they are interested in student employment on campus. If a student does not indicate her interest in a job on the initial form, based on her eligibility, work-study can be added later on if funds are available. Finally, students are awarded funds based on their particular level of need, the funds their institution is able to provide, and the date that they apply.

## Nonfederal Work-Study

Students who have not been awarded work-study seek employment off campus, resulting in costs incurred for transportation and the extra worry of careful scheduling. It is more desirable, especially for first-year students, to have a job on campus as they acclimate themselves to their new environment. A job on campus gives most students more flexibility by concentrating their activities in one place. My university is often willing to grant "institutional work-study" to a student who has a special skill, talent, need, or prior training for a job that he or she is applying for. In my own case, I use this option sparingly because of the surfeit of students who qualify for work-study. In one case, I had a student whose parents' financial situation improved significantly, disqualifying her from continuing her work-study position. She was entering her junior year and loved her library job. I requested and received institutional work-study for her and am happy that I did. She is now in her final year of library school!

## Hourly Pay Rates

These will vary from institution to institution. At my university, most students can expect to start out making minimum wage with incremental increases each year. The pay is far from lavish and they won't be able to contribute to their retirement plan or receive insurance benefits, but the hours are flexible and the location, needless to say, is convenient!

## Student Work Eligibility Requirements

Surprisingly, many students are unaware of the fact that they have a work-study allotment and do not seek employment on campus. Conversely, often those who do not have work-study will be eager to work!

The writing of any student hiring practices for your library should contain a policy on hiring students who are seeking an institutional allotment (Nonfederal Work-Study). There may be valid reasons, though, not to ask for an institutional allotment. A few years ago, my own institution had an unprecedented surfeit of students with work-study allotments on a waiting list for jobs on campus. Our Enrollment Management Department asked that departments on campus hire only students with work-study allotments. Campus departments responded by taking on extra students in some cases, creating positions for students. Not until all of those students were hired would they consider those who sought an institutional allotment. It was a concerted effort and a fair practice, since those who had work-study had demonstrated need.

## Rehiring Students

Before the end of each semester, have a meeting with all of your students to determine their suitability for the following semester. This process is really not as labor-intensive as it sounds, because, ideally and depending on the number of students you have working for you, you will have a very good idea if the student has been meeting the library's expectations and you will have been guiding them and providing feedback throughout.

A few years ago I hired a student who was recommended to me by a faculty member. She was a transfer student looking for on-campus employment. I met with her and liked her a lot, though I noticed a bit of shyness. She performed her duties competently at the circulation desk, but decidedly did not favor contact with other people. I had to consistently remind her that she needed to be aware of every person who walked through the library doors and that greeting them, even if it was only with a smile, was simply good customer service. I had noticed this and so had my colleagues and others, because most students enjoy the opportunity to engage with those coming into the library. On one occasion, a professor had to rap on the circulation desk to get her attention. I explained to her how important, and, in fact, how very basic it was to simply look up and greet everyone who entered. She was always absorbed in the latest *People* magazine or *Cosmopolitan*, with her head down, her hair like a curtain and her face practically on the page. Predictably, she went on the defensive when I gave her feedback, and then she said she'd do much better in the upcoming semester. I had decided, though, that I had given her more than ample time to correct her behavior. In fact, due to depending on her during two busy shifts, I delayed actually taking action longer than I should have.

As long as we are being up-front with what we expect from students right from the beginning and they know what is expected of them, we are within our rights as their employers to terminate them due to not meeting expectations. Usually when I relieve a student of her duties (and, yes, sometimes it is a relief to the student!), it is because of a consistent problem that I have already discussed with the student and, for one reason or another, she has been unable or unwilling to correct it.

## Conclusion

The details of hiring and training students mimic the hiring and training done in the "real world," only on a smaller, more contained scale. All these steps are important for the obvious reasons, in addition to the process in and of itself being a wonderful training ground for what students will experience in their search for jobs off campus and upon graduation.

Holding students to standards, emphasizing accountability, teaching them to be a part of the whole, tapping into their unique talents and strengths, and giving them the support they need to fully realize their own potential is a unique responsibility of the librarian working with students in the academic library setting. It is not easy. You will have your days, they will have theirs, but this is to be expected. I often tell students that a library job may be the kindest that they will ever have and I urge them to learn all they can from it. In the end, the beautiful thing is, if you are really paying attention, you will learn from them, too.

# Cultural and Other Considerations

**Many and Varied**

*There never were in the world two opinions alike, no more than two*
*hairs or two grains; the most universal quality is diversity.*
—Michel de Montaigne

*In our work and in our living we must recognize that difference is a reason*
*for celebration and growth rather than a reason for destruction.*
—Audre Lorde

*Like farmers we need to learn that we cannot sow and reap the same day.*
—Anonymous

ONE OF THE nicer aspects of working in an academic library is the variety of students with whom one has the opportunity to work. In this chapter *cultural* will take on different meanings, as it can, in the context of students, allude to a number of situations. Patience and understanding will be valuable tools for the librarian working with these differences. For instance, on my campus, our international students represent nearly forty different countries. Along with their hopes and desire for a quality education, they bring their culture, the very core of who they are. Moreover, some of the students who come to study at our university from other parts of the United States bring their regional sensibilities with them: those from the West Coast really do tend to be more laid back and those from the Midwest tend to be polite to a fault—and both tend to be surprised by the forthrightness of the East Coast mentality! First-generation students present another aspect of student culture. All of these different "groups" present unique situations to be aware of and strategies that can be specifically targeted to them. All in all, the great equalizer among students is that all are subject to the same rules, environment, and so on. They may react differently, cope differently, and succeed or fail depending on the emotional, cultural, or educational background they come from. Many of the things discussed here, as they apply to different groups, can be said to be representative of the student body at large, proving perhaps that, though we are all different at our core, we are, in many ways, the same, too.

I have always felt that all aspects of a student's culture should be taken into careful consideration when training them for work in the library, but more importantly when mentoring them. In fact, sensitivity to a student's cultural differences is a very clear-cut example of when the librarian must manage his or her expectations of how a student will not only perform the duties assigned but also view your authority and show her receptiveness to mentoring.

This involves dismissing preconceptions and involves a large amount of understanding as to how certain cultural (and, I might add, gender) differences might inhibit, even temporarily, a student's ability to acclimate himself to a particular work style in the same way that another student would.

## Various Modes of Communication

Employing a nonthreatening attitude is a good way to ease students into the job. If your style is naturally a brisk and no-nonsense one, this could inhibit a student's ability to grasp aspects of training, most particularly in the case of, say, international students. An American student may not think twice about such an attitude (or, then again, she may), but will be better equipped culturally to know that it is not an indictment of her own character. The social culture on most U.S. campuses is rather casual, with students often addressing their professors or others in a position of authority by their first names—a strict departure from the norms of previous generations. This is often shocking to an international student, who may feel that being "friendly" with one's professor has no function in his learning experience, whereas an American student may tend to feel more "accepted," enabling him to ease himself into a new experience. The rest of the world may be mystified by the American concept of friendliness—asking perfect strangers "How are you?" and actually expecting an answer! I have always thought it interesting when pairing students to work together at the circulation desk to observe how they size each other up—how an American student will feel a foreign student is, for instance, "inscrutable" and how a foreign student might perceive an American student as "loud," "intrusive," or "insincere" since the American student affords everyone the same casual level of friendliness. I have often mediated these cultural differences on both sides and realize that things unfold in their own time. Eventually, students come around to understanding one another.

I, too, have had to shift my thinking in more ways than one. I have had to assert, ever so gently, my authority over the students who tend to get a bit too casual with me, my colleagues, or their job in general. Conversely, I have also had to ease the grip of "respect" my students from other cultures wish to bestow upon me. I have been called "teacher," "boss," "Madame," and even, quite disconcertingly and unexplainably, "Sir"! I have experienced embarrassment in being deified in such a way—I and my colleagues are not used to this! Indeed, though, I have had to inform a student from Louisiana (good southern manners) that calling me "ma'am" was not necessary—and that the use of my first name was just fine!

The point must be made, though, that most if not all African, Asian, and Middle Eastern countries' youth (and others) treat their elders—most particularly parents and teachers—with great respect and deference. To do otherwise would be unthinkable. It takes time to ease students out of such extreme respect, but the goal would be to find some middle ground. While we want our students to feel comfortable and be their authentic selves, such deference often puts them out of step in their environment, and they very much want (and, in fact, need) to blend into their environment. I have witnessed the slow transformation of behaviors—it is an amazing thing. It just takes time. I always try to instruct students (no matter what their cultural orientation) gently, in ways that do not call undue attention to differences that have the potential to embarrass them greatly. To the student who called me "Madame" I simply said, "Call me Michelle, please." Then I went on to joke "I love to hear the sound of my own name!" This was returned with a giggle. Much to my relief, she never called me "Madame" again.

Proceeding at a slower pace with students who have come from places where different work and social behaviors are in place is in order. Students are already trying to decipher so much about a new environment, the stress level is bound to be sky high. Presuming, too, that students will all be working with at least one other student during their shift (not to mention they will already be totally immersed in campus/dorm life), students will catch on, in time, by observing the behavior of the other students around them. They will learn a new way to communicate, a new way to "be," that will more often than not be the middle way between both styles.

I learned early on that many students, no matter where they come from, can be caught off guard by my cheerful (most of the time!) and relaxed conversational style. Some have perceived this as a certain crossing of boundaries of friendly intimacy (for lack of a better term) that they felt was never established in the first place. During your time with your work-study students, there will be opportunities to get to know them and mentor them along the way. Presenting yourself in the kind but traditional authority role will help them fit in and, at least initially, feel more comfortable. Authorities and experts on nearly every college and university campus are well equipped to handle problems of adjustment and other difficulties that may arise with any student, no matter where they come from. Referring students to the appropriate campus office and professionals, should a problem arise, is not only desirable, but makes good sense too.

## Not Like Home

Students are going through a myriad of feelings, among them homesickness and culture shock. Other troubles range from having roommate problems, feeling overwhelmed by a class load, and worrying about money, to hating the food. When the excitement of seeing one's friends again and feeling that breath of freedom from being away from home (for returning students) or the exhilaration of orientation with leaders who are animated and friendly wears off and the real business of settling in becomes all too apparent, issues may manifest themselves in very different ways, depending on the student and the situation. The homesick student may look tired or appear to set about her work in a lackadaisical way. Students may have a faraway look about them, seem not focused, or seem on the verge of tears. The student experiencing culture shock may look angry or become uncommunicative out of the fear of committing social faux pas. Other students may overcommit themselves in an effort to appear agreeable and involved, and then find themselves unable to fulfill those promises and now fear losing face or, worse, friends (especially newfound ones). This can be especially true in the case of, say, international students, for whom saying "no" to a request would seem highly disagreeable. This can be very perplexing and unsettling. If their American contemporaries do not understand the origin of their behavior, such behavior can cause them to become alienated from the very people they long to make a connection with.

## Time Is Relative; or Is It?

Like it or not, time is a commodity in our world, particularly in American culture where our nomenclature is full of phrases that reinforce this. "Time is money!" is something we have heard countless times in our lives—and may have uttered it ourselves. We prize punctuality (and, indeed, are judged by it) even if we, ourselves, sometimes don't observe the standard. Many of us have an arsenal of excuses at the ready when we are late for work, for dental appointments, for paying our bills on time, and so forth.

Students often have an uneasy relationship with time, particularly when it comes to work. One of the most annoying aspects of my job supervising students is being the "timekeeper." Often, students will show up late and leave early. Often excuses are offered, doctor appointments materialize, emergencies at home occur, stomach aches develop—you get the idea. I have long ago given up trying to extract the truth from excuses and outright lies. In the end, it is not really important. But now I do four things that I really feel help students to learn how showing up, putting in your time, and not leaving your shift unless it is a matter of national security are important parts of being a responsible worker.

- I set expectations of what is expected in terms of time, immediately, when hiring a student.
- I consistently reinforce the importance of showing up on time and leaving at the previously agreed time.
- I make very clear the implications for lateness. And I follow through.
- I praise promptness.

For instance, for students from countries or cultures where time is not strictly observed, where the wristwatch is an ornament or not worn at all, where just showing up, though not necessarily *when,* is the important thing, tardiness will be a hard habit to break, but break it they must.

I had the unfortunate experience of having to gently nudge, remind, reprimand, and then, ultimately, let go two students with whom I really enjoyed working for both habitual and excessive lateness. One of them, a male student, always apologized in a very profuse way, though not once ever provided an actual reason or excuse. He would smile, quite sweetly, and say "Okay! Sorry!" Clearly he enjoyed the job and I thought that the threat of losing the job would put an end to his lateness—why would he jeopardize a job that he loved? One final warning was issued in very clear terms, which he violated on his next shift. He was still cheerful after he was let go, said that he understood, and asked me to promise him there would be no "hard feelings" between us! He now has another job on campus where, so far, they are more tolerant of his rather blithe spirit.

The other, a female student from another country, missed a few shifts (without finding a replacement) and would often show up an hour or two late—enough time for me to think, quite reasonably, that she would not be showing up at all. When she was let go, she accepted the decision with respect but was clearly confused about why it was such a big deal in the first place. While I could have stuck it out with these students, I wasn't doing them any favors by tolerating blatantly transgressive behavior, not to mention the fundamental unfairness to students who *were* actually showing up on time and were watching and waiting to see how I might handle the lateness.

I have learned that not being "tolerant" of students' time issues, the most common being habitual lateness, and firmly reinforcing the rules and setting higher expectations of students helps them both in their job in the library and in other aspects of their lives as well. All students working in the academic library setting should have their feet firmly planted on the same level playing field. We can begin our best work with students when we make them aware of the fact that deliberately breaking rules or otherwise engaging in a liberal interpretation of them will have clear consequences.

## First-Generation Students

I have added a section on first-generation students here because, while I believe that issues that arise when mentoring and training a student run the gamut no matter what the student's particular situation, there are exceptions that require another level of understanding. Given the fact that most jobs now require a college education, *at least,* colleges and universities will likely see an increase in applications of first-generation students. While a disproportionate number of these students will apply to, be accepted by, and attend community colleges, their presence will be seen on nearly every campus, both college and university.[1]

First-generation students are defined as those students who are the first in their family to get a college education. This group is unique in that they often lack a network of family members who can pass on the "culture" of college or higher education as far as time management, living away from home, choosing classes, and so on, go. This new experience can seem daunting at best and can plummet self-confidence, especially in the beginning as the students may perceive everyone else as knowing exactly what to do, how to act, and how to "be," except for them. I don't mean to paint this group with so wide a brush, but being cognizant of these issues with the students early on will help the librarian to calibrate how to proceed when mentoring them.

These students will need more guidance and encouragement to avail themselves of everything the campus has to offer. They should be encouraged to work on campus, become involved in extracurricular activities, regularly attend classes, and plan a study schedule that they will stick to. Being attentive to the signs of difficulty with these students can make all the difference between a successful on-campus work experience, with all of its attendant benefits to both the student and the library, and a failed or aborted work experience. We do not work in a vacuum with our students, but instead are part of a campus team, made up of qualified professionals who can work with these students.

## The Danger of Making Assumptions

I have learned by experience that making assumptions about students is a dangerous business and not a very smart thing to do. Appearances can be (and often are) deceptive. Examine some of your own assumptions. Do you think that every Asian student is a math whiz or a pre-med major? A male with gentler tendencies is gay? A student who seems "out of it" may be a victim of drug abuse? A tattooed student is "up to no good"? I have learned to take students at face value. They reveal themselves slowly when trust has been built up over time, most often when they begin to feel comfortable and acclimated in their environment. But even their self-revelation will vary in degrees, and much of that will depend, too, on how you relate to them. The fear of the "authority" figure will be present in many of them—and surprisingly in some, not at all!

A colleague of mine was confused about the gender of one of our students. We discussed how confusing it was because the student gave no clue, either way, as to gender and even had a unisex name. My colleague simply asked the student which "pronoun" was preferred. The student sighed with relief and told her. Both my colleague and I were entirely wrong about which gender we assumed the student was.

In another incident, a few years ago, I confronted a student who was working up front behind the circulation desk, asking her to remove a rather large button she wore on her sweater that represented a personal and rather unusual sexual proclivity. She inclined her head toward me and asked me if her sexuality bothered me. Her boldness should not have startled me, but in that instance it did. She then went on to suggest that maybe it was in fact (ahem!) "a generational hang-up." The memory of the interaction makes me, even at the present moment, blush deeply—her sexuality was the furthest thing from my mind. I chose my words carefully (another teaching moment!) and explained to her that I was not making a judgment on her sexuality or anyone else's. It was a library policy (applicable to both regular employees and student workers) which mandated that no buttons, T-shirts, or anything else that showed advocacy or political statements should be worn *while working behind the circulation desk.* She did as she was asked to do and she removed the button, sulked for a while, feeling as though her rights had been squashed. Eventually, she forgot about the incident and we moved past it. I am still in contact with this student and on one visit back to the library she actually brought up the incident and we both laughed about it—something that was much easier to do from the distance of time and perspective than it was in the actual moment. This story exemplifies the fact that students are not fully formed—nor should they be, during their college years. We have to manage our expectations of their intellectual and emotional growth—they will get there—in their own time. We can help and guide them, but expecting them to understand things from the perspective that we, as grown and experienced working professionals, understand is a prescription for anger and resentment on the part of everyone.

It is better to gently guide and let the student's experiences unfold. Ultimately, allowing students to be who they are is of the utmost importance, and, at the same time, we need to show them what appropriate and professional behavior in the workplace is. In fact, it is both our duty and our responsibility.

Pushing boundaries is part of the process of growing up and one that those who are finding or forging an identity will, developmentally, almost always need to engage in. Everyone working with students will have to gauge his or her own threshold for this type of incident. I am comfortable being challenged, which I believe is a good thing, since given the nature of my position and the number of students that I supervise, I am challenged with alarming regularity! I used to believe that this was, perhaps, some sort of deficiency on my part, that there was something in me that was not authoritative enough, not, God forbid, professional enough. A kind, former colleague of mine disabused me of this notion, however. She reframed my perception of myself by saying, quite simply, that I was a good listener, patient, and "approachable." These are good qualities for any mentor to possess, though our students just may see it in us before we perceive it in ourselves.

In the big picture, it is probably counterproductive to the mentoring relationship to be heavy-handed in any way: to come off as entirely authoritative or present yourself as the "expert" may be just as counterproductive as killing a student with kindness. It is better to find, as much as you can, a balance between the two for the best results. Best to be that "trusted guide," as *Merriam-Webster* so aptly defined *mentor*.

## Strategies

- Understand and acknowledge "cultural" and circumstantial differences.
- Be alert to signs that a student needs or is asking for help.
- Teach students coping strategies and time management techniques. Encourage them to ask for help if those strategies do not work for them.
- Introduce them to other students in the workplace and partner them, at least initially, on tasks and projects.
- Hold a student to workplace standards, but at the same time, help him get there.
- Make your expectations clear and reinforce the way things need to be done; then give them a reasonable amount of time to learn both the tasks and the appropriate behaviors in the professional environment.
- Make sure that students understand that we are free to be who we are in our lives, but that some conformity will usually be expected in the workplace. While we are "on the clock" we must fall in line with the rules (restrictive as we sometimes perceive them to be) of our workplace.
- Often you may not be the best mentor for the student for any number of reasons. Reach out to other faculty or colleagues when you believe that a student could be better mentored by someone else.
- Strength is built on diversity. In a variety of ways this has been proven over and over. Having the opportunity to work with students who vary in culture, opinions, sexual orientation, or any other way under the sun expands our worldview in an invaluable way. We

are all ultimately better for it. As you model tolerance and patience under different circumstances and allow the proper amount of time for your students to acclimate and acculturate themselves, they, in turn, will be more likely to do the same for one another.

## Conclusion

I have had the opportunity to deal with a great number of students possessing a wide variety of differences over the years, but I have learned to focus more on the commonalities that unite us. Each and every one of us is working toward a goal, and while the goal may be different to each of us, it almost always involves a measure of dedication, hard work, and the ability to step out of our comfort zones. Working with others on your campus can help students who may be experiencing the difficulty of adjusting to changes, no matter what they are. As a librarian and mentor to these students, you will encounter them in a totally different way in the library, as their supervisor, than their professor will in the classroom. That is a golden opportunity.

Librarians working with students whom they intend to mentor should be conscious of the effects that gender, race, economic status, and previous educational experiences may have had on student attitudes toward learning in general and work in particular.

What they learn at your hands has the great potential to cut across all areas of their social and academic lives, grounding them in a supportive environment and positioning them for great well-being and success.

### NOTE

1. Steven Zwerling and Howard London, eds., "First Generation Students: Confronting the Cultural Issues," *New Directions for Community Colleges*, no. 80 (1992).

### RESOURCES

Cushman, Kathleen. "Facing the Culture Shock of College." *Educational Leadership* 64, no. 7 (2007): 44–47.

Harper, Shaun R., and Stephen J. Quaye, eds. *Student Engagement in Higher Education: Theoretical Perspectives*. New York: Routledge, 2009.

Inkleas, Karen K., Zaneeta E. Daver, Kristen E. Vogt, and Jeannie B. Leonard. "Living-Learning Programs and First-Generation College Students' Academic and Social Transition to College." *Research in Higher Learning* 48, no. 4 (2007): 403–34.

Kathman, Jane M., and Michael D. Kathman. "What Difference Does Diversity Make in Managing Student Employees?" *College and Research Libraries* 59, no. 4 (1998): 378–89.

Pascarella, Ernest T., Christopher T. Pierson, Gregory C. Wolniak, and Patrick T. Terenzini. "First-Generation College Students: Additional Evidence on College Experiences and Outcomes." *Journal of Higher Education* 75, no. 3 (2004): 249–84.

Redmond, Sonjia P. "Mentoring and Cultural Diversity in Academic Settings." *American Behavioral Scientist* 34, no. 2 (1990): 188–200.

"Roadblocks to International Student Success." *National On-Campus Report* 33, no. 16 (2005): 3–6.

# 5

# Partnering with the Educational Process

*If we are together nothing is impossible. If we are divided all will fail.*
—Winston Churchill

THOSE OF US who work with students in an academic environment are fortunate: we have common goals for all students, among which is to nurture self-confidence in each student and success in their endeavors. Because we all have common goals for students, we can consult with one another and develop strategies for working with particular students who may be struggling in any number of ways. But a student doesn't always have to be struggling for the network of campus professionals to actually work.

Successful students are usually those who are well-integrated into the "full college experience," as so many of us have heard time and time again. What exactly does this mean? It means that students cannot maintain a balanced and reasonably happy or successful college experience if, for instance, they throw their existence out of whack by excessive partying or deciding it is worth it to grab more hours at their on- or off-campus jobs. Even though it would seem to defy logic, a student who spends all of his or her time studying, to the exclusion of everything else, is at risk for different reasons.

Just as nutritionists, in their wisdom, have been forever preaching the rewards and benefits of a balanced diet, the balance of campus life for students is vitally important. Everything in measure. Often family or societal pressures will cause a student to hide himself away, hitting the books relentlessly or otherwise doing things that are out of character. He may begin to feel unequal to the amount of study required, may not feel "smart" enough, or may begin to suffer ill health or engage in behaviors that relieve stress in the short term while creating very real long-term problems.

In a busy library that employs a large number of students it is often extremely difficult (and, frankly, unrealistic) to think that we can zero in on the needs of every student we work with, let alone be cognizant of every difficulty they might be experiencing. It is helpful for the librarian to build relationships with other offices on campus so that student issues can be handled in the most professional and expedient way possible. Referring to other professionals on campus should not be seen as "fobbing off" a student and his problems onto someone else, but rather as engaging in what most librarians refer to as the "handoff"—a behavior that acknowledges when something is beyond our immediate capabilities. And keeping in mind that it is not about us, but rather what is best for the student, will underscore that we have made the right decision. No one works in a vacuum on campus.

While you can check in often, initiate conversations with students about work, school, or any other number of topics, and offer feedback on their job performance, often you will know only what they are willing or able to tell you. The boundary that exists between supervisor and student employees is often one that is not fixed and may be one of extremes: the student who tells all and then some stands in contrast to the student who is so self-contained, for whatever reason, that he or she will never tell you anything except what you may want to hear. For the latter, everything is always "Fine." This is particularly stressful when you have good reason to believe otherwise.

Whoever thought that gently integrating a student who works with you into campus life would be one of your obligations as a librarian? One can imagine collective eye-rolling as busy professionals throw up their hands and reject the role of parent to young adults they have not given birth to! The truth is that mentoring a student is to be a trusted guide to that student. The potential impact we can have in a relationship that may have begun in an informal way is truly tremendous. An anecdote from my own experience can illustrate this point.

A few years ago, I hired a female, first-year student who was very specific about the hours she wanted: Friday evenings and Saturday nights. In the fall semester, meeting her for the first time, I found her a bit standoffish, but polite. The second semester she opened up a bit and asked for more responsibility. Over that summer she initiated a few e-mail conversations with me about some ideas she had for the library. I eventually realized why she chose the hours she did: she had few friends and no social life to speak of. At the start of her sophomore year, she asked to have the same hours. I told her she could have one or the other, but not both. She smiled. She knew exactly what I was doing. I had encouraged her to take small steps to get involved in things on campus, to come out of her room on Saturday nights, and to share something interesting with me that was new and campus-related in her life. But I dangled a carrot of sorts over her head. She coveted the night supervisor shift on Friday evenings. We were only open until 7:00 p.m. and her shift started at 5:00 p.m. It seemed to mean the world to her. I told her that while I thought she would make a fine student supervisor in time, she wasn't there yet. I told her that her inability to make eye contact and her reticence to chat, informally, with the students whose books she checked out at the desk would impede her ability to give directives at the circulation desk. But, and this is important, I didn't say "no."

I encouraged her to work on the very aspects that would make a good supervisor, such as clear communication with others, and told her that we would "revisit" her request. She was an intelligent and sensitive girl, but she was clearly deflated. I saw that immediately but resisted the urge to assure her she would be fine. I wanted, in fact needed, her to take charge of her own experience. I wanted to give her something to strive for. She, like most (if not all) students during the college years, was a work in progress. I wish I could say that this student became an overnight success: outgoing, a leader and a calculated risk-taker, but that would be untrue and rather fantastical. But she certainly became more confident than she was before, and she slowly and steadily integrated herself into a few clubs on campus and even began eating dinner with her roommates during the week. She also struck up a wonderful relationship with a part-time librarian who worked the short shift on those Friday evenings. This librarian took the student "under her wing" and encouraged her in a variety of ways. Interestingly, the student was a bit shy about telling me how well she got along with the other librarian, jokingly telling me "I feel like I'm cheating on you!" I, on the other hand, was thrilled that she was reaching out to other faculty members, whose impact on her was clearly positive. I encouraged her to find others, in a variety of places on campus, with whom she felt comfortable conversing.

I was not at all interested in making her into something that she was not. However, I was very interested in making her better than she was, simply because she had the potential (I could see it!) and she deserved it. During the second semester of her sophomore year, she became that supervisor and executed her duties like a shining star every Friday evening from 5:00 p.m. to 7:00 p.m. In fact, she held that position until she graduated. When we said goodbye to one another on graduation day, she hugged me and said, "I *owned* Friday night, didn't I?" And in a way, she really did. And while I would like nothing better than to think that, eventually, she would have gotten to where she needed to be on her own, I know that my guidance helped. First-year students are particularly vulnerable for a wide variety of reasons. Taking a student in hand, sponsoring him or her, if you will, can make a huge difference. Moreover, it just might tip the balance between a student staying at a school where he or she has at least one mentoring relationship or leaving because of a lack of one.

## What Partnering Really Means

Partnering with the educational process means working from where you are, as a professional on campus, as well as helping to integrate (and refer) students among and to other offices on campus.

Students are constantly learning outside of the classroom. School clubs, sports, and volunteer work are only some of the options for students on campus. Students who learn to balance their time between classes, study, activities, and jobs feel the most satisfaction. When students can manage to create a balance for themselves (which may look very different from the kind of balance we would create for ourselves), this could very well engender a sense of belonging in their environment because everything falls into place and they feel in control of their own lives.

What a student learns, with you as a guide in the library, becomes a stepping-stone to classroom application and vice versa: trust-building, risk-taking, sharpening of skills, and learning professional standards are life skills. The college classroom and an on-campus job, such as working in the library, are wholly appropriate places to both learn and hone the skill set they will need to be good students, self-actualized individuals, and successful future professionals.

## Strategies

- Be cognizant of what your limitations are regarding the student you are mentoring. When and how would your student best benefit from "outside" help?

- Understand that part of mentoring is doing the "handoff" in certain situations, when certain student issues can be handled professionally and expediently.
- Encourage the student to develop relationships outside of the library, or introduce her to others with whom she may share a common interest.

# Conclusion

When we develop meaningful relationships with students, we would like to think that we alone can influence them in a myriad of ways—all for their betterment. But, in fact, we ourselves do not function that way, and this is a misguided way of beginning the process of mentoring. I myself gain valuable insight into my job by consulting with my colleagues, connecting over discussion lists, and going to conferences. We have to encourage our students to make connections with not only our colleagues in the library, but as well with their professors, their peers, and their families. When we have a tooth that throbs and aches, we consult our dentist—quickly—because we are wise enough to know that we cannot extract our own teeth. Often, we can get caught up in our own sense of importance and in the satisfying idea of being able to positively influence students, but, as my own boss, in her infinite wisdom, consistently reminds me and my colleagues, "*It's not about us.*" And while we know that, it doesn't hurt to be reminded!

## RESOURCES

Bova, Breda Murphy, and Rebecca R. Phillips. "The Mentoring Relationship as an Educational Experience." Paper presented at the National Conference of the Adult Education Association, San Antonio, Texas, November 1982.

Kuh, G. D. "Guiding Principles for Creating Seamless Learning Environments for Undergraduates." *Journal of College Student Development* 37, no. 2 (1996): 135–48.

Reinarz, Eric R., and Alice G. White, eds. *Beyond Teaching and Mentoring.* San Francisco: Jossey-Bass, 2001.

Schroeder, C. C., and J. C. Hurst. "Designing Learning Environments That Integrate Curricular and Co-Curricular Experiences." *Journal of College Student Development* 37, no. 2 (1996): 174–81.

Tinto, V. "Classrooms as Communities: Exploring the Educational Character of Student Persistence." *Journal of Higher Education* 68, no. 6 (1997): 599–633.

Zekeri, A. A. "College Curriculum Competencies and Skills Former Students Found Essential to Their Careers." *College Student Journal* 38, no. 3 (2004): 412–22.

# 6

# Engaging Students

## The Library as Learning Lab

*Only connect.*
—E. M. Forster

*Self-absorption in all its forms kills empathy, let alone compassion. When we focus on ourselves, our world contracts as our problems and preoccupations loom large. But when we focus on others, our world expands. Our own problems drift to the periphery of the mind and so seem smaller, and we increase our capacity for connection—or compassionate action.*
—Daniel Goleman

THERE IS A copious amount of literature that discusses the importance of student engagement in academia. We know that students who are engaged in their experiences are more likely to be happy and successful students. Because as librarians we will meet students who are at various stages of acclimation and training in the job in the library, we will be called upon to develop different strategies for dealing with them as individuals.

We can help students to see their job in the library as an extension of the classroom, a learning lab, if you will, where they will learn skills that will extend way beyond the classroom and their college experience.

All students who work in the library are ambassadors of sorts. They may have one idea of the library as a student and a whole other one as a student worker. Those student workers go out into the campus community and will share their impressions of the library as place, thus influencing other students' perceptions and, by extension, their use of the library. Librarians play a very large part in these perceptions by how we engage the students we meet by chance at the reference desk or in the classroom or by working with those we hire. What we have the opportunity to do is to build relationships, not just have interactions. We can be the tipping point for students who are unprepared for the college experience for many different reasons and for those who find themselves capable, though adrift. We should be thinking of relationships with students that will endure.

## What Is Student Engagement?

To understand the key to student engagement, it is important to know two outstanding features of the process:[1]

- Student effort—the amount of time and effort students put into any (educational) activity
- The efforts of those around the students, such as faculty—through educational activities, opportunities, support services, and social interactions

Put together, all of these factors will influence the quality of a student's academic experience, which in turn influences how successful the student will be.

The nature and frequency of our interactions with students have a great impact on student success. For instance, when we engage students in discussions about their classes, their assignments, their career plans, or other aspects of their college experience, we are often providing them with a well-needed sounding board, valuable and instant feedback, needed validation, and suggestions or strategies. Students who work with us can benefit greatly from our counsel both academically and job-wise. When we show interest and engage those who encounter us by chance, at their point of need, in the library, students benefit in two ways. They come to see the library as an important institution on campus, an appropriate and viable place to serve their academic and research needs. Students also benefit by getting to know a "go to" person in the library. Knowing a librarian is a wonderful entrée for students who lack vital academic connections on campus, and it can help ease any library anxiety they may have.

In my own library two years ago, I encountered an inordinate number of students who seemed incredibly happy to be working in the library, pleased to have found work that they truly enjoyed. They would constantly approach me with new ideas for attracting students to our services and participated with gusto in the planning of different events such as National Library Week. I had asked them if they would be interested in starting a library club or a student advisory board. I didn't have to say anything else. Within three weeks they, with my help, had laid the groundwork, done the research, and consulted with all of the appropriate people to be able to get the advisory board together, including choosing officers, setting up an institutional account, and writing a mission statement and bylaws. I urged them to set up meetings with the library director as well as the chief information officer of the library so that they could reach out, in a professional way, to let them know that they were working hard to advocate on behalf of the students.

Engaging the students in this type of professional and educational activity has been particularly gratifying for me and has been a boon to the self-confidence of all of the students involved. Having students start this group provided an extra level of work for me, as well, though I did not mind in the least. Three of the students who have since graduated expressed interest in somehow still being involved in the group as alumni. The student advisory board is considering their request!

## Strategies

- Encourage students to engage in campus functions and try to accommodate their request, within reason, to do so, if that should clash with their work hours.
- Acculturate students to the culture of the library and, in turn, teach *them* how to engage with others whom they will encounter while they are working. Engagement engenders engagement.
- Engage them in their ideas and allow them to explore options. Learning to say "yes" to a student's request to explore an idea further and then providing the tools as well as the moral support will help them to take further risks. They might even succeed!
- Keep connected by engaging them in frequent conversations about their classes, their areas of study, and their grades.
- Don't be afraid to disclose something of yourself and your own "story." I was (and continue to be) shy as a student, quiet, and a risk-taker, but only in my mind. Students laugh when they hear that, as they try to reconcile that image with the one in front of them. I tell them about why I was an English major, how I got into librarianship, my experience working in a public library, and the differences between that kind of library and the academic library. That exchange of information is an essential component of engaging the student and prevents the relationship from being uneven. Students are more

likely to share something of themselves when others are willing to do the same.

- Taking the time to work side by side with a student, for instance, straightening books in the stacks, or sitting at the circulation desk with them, or otherwise asking them for their help with a task, will provide a more nonthreatening and natural conversation with them. They are likely to open up more if you are not gazing down at them from behind your desk, in your office. Conversations should happen easily and spontaneously—they do not have to be scheduled.

## Conclusion

Engaging students and keeping them engaged has far-reaching implications for student success in higher education. Seeing students as young adults, real people rather than simply blank slates waiting to be written words of wisdom on, is something everyone working with them would do well to remember. In many instances we are so focused on everything we need to do as professionals to educate them and mold them that we fail to realize that they come to us with already formed thoughts, feelings, desires, and fears. As librarians we can work with students in order to lead them to the best resources for their research, inculcate search strategies in them, and instruct them in the ways of technology—thus reducing library anxiety, an affliction many of them have—but we can do even more. We can engage them in the classroom. In the cafeteria. At school events. At library orientations. But we can do even more than that. We can see them as young people who are also eager to let us know something of themselves, as people who have had ideas and opinions before they came to us. If we listen well enough, they just might come back to continue the conversation. Or even start a new one.

## NOTE

1. Larry Hardesty, ed., *The Role of the Library in the First College Year*, The First-Year Experience Monograph Series no. 45 (Columbia: University of South Carolina Press, 2007), 19.

## RESOURCES

Harper, Shaun R., and Stephen J. Quaye, eds. *Student Engagement in Higher Education: Theoretical Perspectives*. New York: Routledge, 2009.

Kuh, George D., Polly D. Boruff-Jones, and Amy E. Mark. "Engaging Students in the First College Year: Why Librarians Matter." In *The Role of the Library in the First College Year* (Monograph no. 45), edited by Larry Hardesty, 17–28. Columbia, SC: University of South Carolina, National Resource Center for the First-Year Experience and Students in Transition, 2007.

Kuh, George D., Jillian Kinzie, John H. Schuh, and Elizabeth J. Whitt. "Student Engagement: A Key to Success." In *Student Success in College: Creating Conditions That Matter*, 7–21. San Francisco: Jossey-Bass, 2010.

# How Students See Their Place in the Library; or, What *Is* Work, Anyway?

*We don't see things as they are; we see them as we are.*

—Anaïs Nin

ALTHOUGH IT MAY sound well-worn and cliché, perspective is everything. So much of what should be obvious simply isn't. What should be simple rarely is. For example, we need students to work. They need a job. It should all fall into place, right? Maybe, but it rarely does. Some basic understanding of the students' position at the outset helps.

When I first began working with students in the library, I thought it was all a very easy equation: hire + train = supervise. I had given no serious thought as to how students saw their place in the library as workers. Employees? Students?

There is no clear delineation between the roles that the student worker plays in the library. What they do blurs the line between student and employee, often leaving supervisors unsure as to how much we can reasonably expect from them in terms of reliability, responsibility, and workload. Clearly students are put in a situation that cannot, on the face of things, inspire confidence. Because of their ambiguous status, they are not subject to the same responsibilities as regular employees, but they also do not have the same recourse should specific problems arise, such as grievance committees, formal and rigorously enforced standards of conduct, and handbooks.[1]

One of the first students I hired had an incredibly cheerful personality and presented herself as a very good worker, and she was assiduous, most especially with the work she was assigned in the stacks. She had her own section, which I had allowed her to choose. She carefully shelf read, dusted, and straightened the books in that section with a regularity that bordered on the compulsive. However, when she returned to the circulation desk, she would pull out her notebooks and her big, heavy biology textbooks, spread them out on the desk in front of her, and hunker down to study. She would effectively ignore the students who came to the desk to check out books or who otherwise needed any kind of assistance. She would let the circulation desk phone ring until a librarian, confused and annoyed, would stop whatever he or she was doing to answer it.

The student was in a world of her own. I was more than a little annoyed at her behavior, which was totally at odds with the powerhouse that she was in the stacks. A few times I gently asked her to put away her books, assuming that she would understand that studying to the exclusion of her duties was unacceptable. She would give me a look of hurt and sincere puzzlement. One day she left the library, seemingly on the verge of tears. It bothered me and I vowed to address the situation with her when she came in for her next scheduled shift. Before I had the chance, she returned later that day and asked to speak with me, privately. I was initially happy that she had seen the error of her ways and was being proactive in coming to me to apologize and to vow to try harder.

Since I didn't have an office at the time, she walked me back to her area in the stacks, the Qs to be specific, and told me how confused she was about her job. When I asked her which aspect of her job, exactly, confused her, she looked at me as though I were dense. She said, "I'm a work-study student, right?" I nodded. "I take care of this section really well, don't I?" she asked, her voice quavering a bit. "You do," I agreed. "Well," she explained, "that's the work part, right?" *Ah.* I saw exactly where she was going. "Yes," I said, smiling to myself. "Right," she said. "So when I go back to the circulation desk, that's the study part, but you are not giving me the chance to do what I need to do and I feel really frustrated."

I understood immediately that her definition of "work-study" was not the same as mine. At first I felt defensive and wondered how a student could possibly *not* see things my way. But, in fact, it was just one of many misconceptions that students will often and understandably have, and it was my job to clear it up. How could they know my conception of their jobs unless I had clearly communicated that at the outset of their employment? This student was an intelligent young woman who was genuinely dismayed at her seeming inability to do the job right, despite all her efforts. She was frustrated at the number of times I told her she could not do something that was clearly sanctioned by her very job title. And that she came to me of her own volition is rare, indeed. Many students simply quit once the frustration builds.

When I explained to her, in a straightforward but kind manner, exactly what was expected of her, she was initially embarrassed that she had misunderstood. I reassured her. We called it a "learning experience." I told her that not only would she have many such experiences, but that I, at my age, was still having them! I also took responsibility for not making it clear to her (and of course, my many other students) exactly what was expected in the library, not only the particulars but, perhaps more importantly, how to *be* a worker and how to *exist* in the workplace. If we need and expect students to be a blessing rather than a burden in the workplace, we need to be explicit about what we expect of them.

## What Is Work, Anyway?

Academic libraries depend quite heavily on student workers, though students often do not have any real understanding of how integral they are to our operation. For instance, students may not think anything of the fact that they miss a shift every once in a while. "What's the big deal?" they might think, since they figure they simply won't get paid as much as they normally do.[2] In my own library, in which two students are scheduled for the circulation desk for every hour that we are open, a student may call out, reasoning that another person is working the shift anyway. Well, as these things usually go, the other student thinks the same thing! I have spent many a morning or afternoon scrambling around trying to find a student who could pick up a shift so that I could get on with attending meetings, teaching classes, and fulfilling any other of a number of responsibilities I have during the day.

When confronted, a student may plead the "family emergency," putting you in the position of not being able to probe further. What causes this behavior? Simply put, they just don't know the culture and expectation of work. *Yet.* But once they know, *they know.* And they will only know if we both tell them and model that behavior. And then they are on notice, after which you must decide what your rules or your threshold for such behavior will be. I will often ask my students to imagine a job in the "real world," where such a cavalier attitude toward something as basic as showing up will not be tolerated. I am, more often than not, met with silence. Because they do not answer does not mean they don't have an answer. The question will definitely give them a point of departure for thinking about their relationship to their job in particular and to work in general.

## Why Do Students Work?

Students may seek employment for a variety of reasons. Students may work because their parents expect them to, or because they want to, or maybe because they simply have to. In some cases, none of these applies, and a student may seek employment because his or her friends are working. Some students will apply for jobs on campus that interest them: an accounting major might seek work in the business office, a psychology student who loves animals might choose to work with lab rats, a math major might work in the tutoring center. And yes, occasionally, a student who loves books will want to work in the library. Often, a student will simply receive a "placement" from the work-study office on campus and show up with only a vague idea of what the job may entail. Our student workers in the library work for us, but are not "employees" in the conventional sense of the word. Their need to work, in most, if not all, cases, is of a supplemental nature. Still, they must learn to create a balance in their lives away from home, including completely new patterns of study, work, and socialization.

## Students Need to Navigate the Transition Phase

The point at which students are often seeking employment for the first time will occur when a myriad of changes are occurring in their lives, destabilizing for a time all they have previously known.[3] Often at the same time that we are expecting students to show up, participate in training, take initiative, and show responsibility, they may be far from home for the first time, left largely to their own devices, and separated from the friends they've had their whole lives, their parents, and their beloved dog or iguana. They have new classes, roommates, and professors who may seem inscrutable. We encounter them in a state of transition, and yet still we expect so much of them. We can help them during this time by acknowledging the changes in their lives, creating clear guidelines for behavior, and, as explicitly as possible, communicating our expectations of them.

## Strategies

- Provide a clearly written job description and go over it with the students.
- Provide a framework for the students' understanding of the importance of their job. For instance, students might not find sitting at the circulation desk particularly important until it is explained to them that they provide the first point of contact for library patrons.
- Give students the opportunity to do a variety of tasks.
- Encourage your colleagues to interact with students. This will prevent the students from feeling as though they exist within their own "silo" in the library.
- Encourage students to talk about their preconceived notions of work and how they see themselves as a student-worker.
- Make them feel integral to the functioning of the library on a daily basis and reward and encourage their efforts.

## Conclusion

Students do not come to us necessarily knowing that they are truly needed in their positions. In fact, they tend to think in terms of what they can get out of a job (money, a recommendation letter, etc.) rather than what they themselves will contribute. In time, these notions can be gently disabused by acculturating the student in the library workplace through frequent conversations with you, as both mentor and supervisor, and with others who are in a position to guide them.

### NOTES

1. Gail V. Oltmans, "The Student Perspective," *Journal of Library Administration* 21, no. 3/4 (1995): 63–76.
2. William K. Black, ed., *Libraries and Student Assistants: Critical Links* (New York: Hayworth, 1995).
3. Judith F. Hammes and Emil J. Haller, "Making Ends Meet: Some of the Consequences of Part-Time Work for College Students," *Journal of College Student Personnel* 16 (1983): 529–35.

## RESOURCES

Constatinon, Constantia. "Recruiting, Training and Motivating Student Assistants in Academic Libraries." *Catholic Library World* 69, no. 1 (1998): 20–23.

Kathman, Jane M., and Michael D. Kathman. "Training Student Employees for Quality Service." *Journal of Academic Librarianship* 26, no. 3 (2000): 176–82.

White, Emilie C. "Student Assistants in the Academic Libraries: From Reluctance to Reliance." *Journal of Academic Librarianship* 11, no. 2 (1985): 93–97.

# Teaching Professional Behavior; or, "Cruel to Be Kind!"

*Cruel to be kind in the right measure*
*Cruel to be kind it's a very good sign*
—Nick Lowe

*A good example has twice the value of good advice.*
—Author unknown

WHILE FAR BE it from me to advocate cruelty in any form, teaching professional behavior can often be uncomfortable for both the mentor and the mentee. In fact, any time that you have to correct students, even in the kindest of ways, they will tend to feel as though you are "going at them." They will not be able to make the immediate connection that you are correcting them because you really want them to do well, because, most of the time, they will sincerely want to please you. And they want to be thought well of, also.

## Teachable Moment(s)

I once had a student who, when working in the library, insisted on speaking to faculty he encountered in an overly familiar way. Once when the president of the university came to the library for a meeting, the student called out to him, "Yo! Dude!" The president, in turn, laughed and waved back. Clearly, the student and the president were familiar with one another, in general a really nice thing to see. The president did not seem at all perturbed by the student's informal greeting. However, I was.

When I took the student aside to speak with him about the incident he laughed, saying that the two of them always joked together. I explained to him that while that may be true, he is working in the library, he represents the library, and the behavior was unprofessional, not only for the obvious reasons, but also because it set a bad example for other students. I made it a condition of his employment that he would apologize to the president for calling him dude. Later in the day, the student came back triumphantly and said that he did, in fact, apologize but that the president waved him off, saying "no big deal."

You are probably wondering what was accomplished, in the end, if the student still did not understand that what he did was inappropriate in the workplace. Consequences. Even if I did not manage to make him understand, I communicated a clear consequence. In this case actions speak louder than words. I, of course, had no intention of threatening him or in any way denigrating him, but he clearly needed to know that what he did was behavior not fitting in the workplace. I presented him with a choice: he could apologize or seek employment elsewhere. It was his decision. It was a teachable moment, and I seized it.

## Strategies

### Situate the Student within the Organization

This was not an obvious point to me until one day I complained to my own boss that some of my students just didn't "get it." She suggested I show them an organizational chart that illustrated how responsibility flowed and how integral the students were to day-to-day functioning.

### Socialize Students to the Workplace

Introduce the students who will be working for you to other professionals and paraprofessionals in the library. It is helpful for them to know all of the other people in the department, while at the same time drawing some boundaries. For instance, I stress to all of my students that staff desks and all of the things on them are strictly off-limits. It is not appropriate to take a pen, use their telephone when they go off to lunch, or go rummaging in their drawers for paper clips. It is, however, okay (and desirable) for them to go to library staff for clarification of duties if their supervisor isn't present or to *ask* if they may borrow something.

### Elicit Questions about Your Job in Particular or
### Librarianship as a Profession in General

Quite often, students do not have an accurate view as to what librarians do all day. The best way to disabuse them of their preconceived notions is to engage them in conversations about the profession and, if time and opportunity arise, have them "shadow" you occasionally. For example, I have occasionally brought work-study students of mine to bibliographic instruction sessions to speak about their own research processes to their peers.

## Model Professional Behavior

This point would seem self-evident, but librarians, like other professionals, are busy with many and varied duties and not always conscious of how they are being perceived by the students who work with and among them. We just need to be cognizant of the fact that we are, without a doubt, being constantly evaluated and judged.

*Be discreet.* Conversations about campus politics, organizational changes, and complaints about coworkers or other students should be conducted in private and away from students. Like the childhood game "whisper down the lane," your one indiscretion may be repeated a thousand times on campus by a work-study student who will relish the "insider" information he heard at work.

*Be on time.* You can hardly expect your students to show up when they are supposed to if you mosey in forty-five minutes late clutching a Starbucks bag and sipping on your mocha latte.

*Teach your students to respect your office space and your time in it.* I have to stress to each new student I hire that when I am meeting in my office with someone and the door is closed, they should seek help from a colleague unless it is an emergency only I can handle. (This has never happened!) I have had students press their faces against the glass door, continuously knock, or, even worse, just walk right in. Letting them know this is unacceptable right away saves them future embarrassment and you a whole lot of irritation.

## Set Expectations for Tasks and Deadlines for Projects

None of us has an ocean of time to complete a task or a project. This is a concept with which students ought to be well aware, since they will often encounter deadlines set by their professors. However, they may only associate deadlines with schoolwork, not yet possessing a clear understanding that those of us in the work environment are also under the familiar pressure of deadlines.

## Provide a Framework for Working Together

Work does not get done in a vacuum and, particularly in a library, not alone. I will often explain to students how the front end of the library (circulation desk) is supported by the back end (acquisitions, collection development, serials, and interlibrary loan) and vice versa. When we all work together, we make one another look good while delivering vital services in a helpful, professional, and expedient way. Teamwork is essential.

## Reinforce Communication Skills

One of my students was taking a class in which she felt like she was the only one who didn't know what was going on. The instructor required that they all participate in a group project, which sent my student into a tailspin. She was incredibly shy and tended to get rather tongue-tied. She felt that she was not welcome in the group she was placed in and wondered what she could contribute. She told me that I was "lucky" that I didn't have to deal with situations like that. Ha! We have all found ourselves at odds with a coworker or the only one at a meeting with a dissenting opinion.

Until it becomes socially acceptable at work to suck your thumb and sulk or throw your food across the cafeteria table, working on our interpersonal skills is a lifelong endeavor. Students need to realize they must listen, acknowledge, and respond, all with respect, even when it is the last thing they want to do. This is a skill that needs constant work, as relationships, by their very nature, are never static: they are in constant flux and people we work with will act differently on different days, all depending on their moods. Helping our students to understand this and to read others' social cues will ease their anxiety, especially when they feel as though they "can't get along with anyone."

## Teach Flexibility

Things change and change is inevitable. Preach this early and often. Encourage students to be open and flexible. We tend not to think of students as being rigid or set in their ways, but college is such a unique experience in and of itself that, when coupled with a campus job, it can feel overwhelming. Many students, especially those far from home, will welcome any opportunity to cling to anything that has become familiar in a new place or situation. Many will long for the relief of being able to complete one task and then go on to the next. I remember one summer giving one of my students the job of revising the student handbook. She enjoyed doing it and spent a lot of time on it. When I saw the finished product, crazy fonts and all, I suggested some changes, some of which were significant. She became very frustrated until I explained to her that a marketing plan I'd been working on for the library had gone through at least eleven significant revisions at the ever-wise insistence of my boss. That's just how it works!

## Conclusion

Acclimating students to the workplace should be a priority in all campus departments where students work. Librarians, as actual professionals, are uniquely positioned to model, teach, and reinforce professional behavior that will benefit students later on. The old saying, "People may not believe what you say, but they will always believe what you do," is full of wisdom and we would do well to take its lesson to heart. These lessons will be like small seeds that we plant, and while we may not immediately or always see the fruits of our efforts in this direction, it is important that we lay the groundwork. Hopefully they will serve as examples to students that they will be able to recall and draw wisdom from in whatever job or professional position they will eventually find themselves in.

### RESOURCES

Liptak, John J. "Using Emotional Intelligence to Help College Students Succeed in the Workplace." *Journal of Employment Counseling* 42 (2005): 171–78.

Wright, Cheryl A., and Scott D. Wright. "The Role of Mentors in the Career Development of Young Professionals." *Family Relations* 36, no. 2 (1987): 204–8.

# Motivation Is a Muscle

*Motivation will almost always beat mere talent.*
—Norman R. Augustine

*Motivation is the art of getting people to do what you want them to do because they want to do it.*
—Dwight D. Eisenhower

MAKE NO MISTAKE about it; motivation is a muscle that must be developed. The lack of it can be one of the most difficult and maddening aspects of working with students in the library. It is an important life skill that can be engendered, but how?

Motivation in a student, while often hard to see, is not, I believe, one of those qualities that a person either has or doesn't have. Every student wants to do well. Every student desires something for himself or herself, and it is a very basic human trait to want to be held in high regard.

A student with whom you work in the library, as stated in an earlier chapter, may be there for a variety of reasons, the least of which may be to be the best library worker he or she can possibly be. So what's next?

Mixed strategies can be employed to increase not only motivation but also initiative in a student worker. Not every strategy will work for every student. Modeling enthusiasm as well as defining clear expectations of the student will lay the groundwork.

## The Intimidation Factor

Often, when we perceive students to be alternately unmotivated, lacking in initiative, or just plain lazy, what we may actually be seeing is the result of anxiety over a first job coupled with a very real inability to understand exactly what is expected of them. It is difficult to remember how incredibly intimidating a grown-up in a position of authority can be. Your position as their boss can be very intimidating no matter how friendly you present yourself to them. The anxiety is often the by-product of having a great desire to succeed and do well but fearing the exact opposite: utter failure and embarrassment.

## Strategies

### Clearly Communicate Expectations

Be as concrete as possible by giving the students tangible goals. For instance, a student working the early morning shift might be told, "Please make sure all of the newspapers are processed first thing. All the computers and printers should be turned on." These are two tasks that must be done in the morning, identified in a clear and direct way.

### Speak in a Way That Folds the Students into the Job

Reinforce the fact that their efforts are for the greater good, that they are part of the larger picture. Elicit their opinions and reactions. Let them be creative. For instance, "Next month is Women's History Month. Would you like to get together a book display?"

### Avoid Favoritism among Your Student Staff

Nobody likes it when a boss plays favorites. Competition can cause doubt and anxiety, which are counterproductive in the workplace and a motivation killer. A student might think, "Why even try, she's obviously better than I am." Each student possesses and brings unique strengths to their position. Exploiting those strengths at every opportunity will increase the likelihood that the students will want to use them.

### Model Interest and Enthusiasm for All Tasks at Hand

Students are experts at picking up subtle cues from the adults around them and will often react accordingly. If you are disgruntled they will begin to feel apathetic and disinterested about their own roles. If you don't care, why should they?

### Build Trust

How, you wonder, could this increase motivation? Increasing trust increases confidence. The students will know that it is okay to try because mistakes will be tolerated. Building trust can be further accomplished when they can function in an atmosphere that is open and honest and where they are consistently encouraged. I like to place students in situations or give them specific tasks to complete that I know they will succeed in. Doing so builds confidence and goodwill, which will then, as a natural extension, slowly build itself into trust.

## Create Challenges

In order to avoid boredom and rote completion of required tasks, challenge students to the next level. In our library, students whose job it is to sit at the circulation desk, for instance, will often experience extremely busy times as well as periods of time when nothing at all is going on. The latter is the time when I and my colleagues will often recruit students to do other tasks for us that engage them on a creative or intellectual level, such as maintaining spreadsheets for statistics, creating subject-specific booklists or book displays, or any other number of tasks that go beyond the usual. After completing the task, solicit their opinion of the task, which will increase their interest and keep them motivated. Make sure to look for opportunities to exploit their interests and their strengths. In this way you will be placing them in situations in which they will succeed.

## Teach Problem Solving

Students will often ask a question instead of figuring out something for themselves. Investing a reasonable amount of time in student training will help to mitigate at least some of the resistance students will have to solving problems on their own, but not all of it. It helps to know that what drains away initiative is often the fear of making a wrong decision. If a student does make a "wrong" decision or one in which there was a much better alternative, take the time to go through the steps taken and look for other possible alternatives. This type of reflection is essential to helping the student process the experience of making mistakes in a nondetrimental way.

## Encourage Decision Making

The work environment is rife with decision making. Every moment of every day we are called upon to make decisions, big or small. Decisions require action, action requires personal responsibility, and being personally responsible can, in some situations, inspire fear or emotional paralysis. When training students it can be really helpful to present them with theoretical scenarios in which they can think through the proper steps they might take to reach a reasonable decision. One of my students let a university trustee, who needed to be let into the executive meeting room where she would be conducting an important interview, wait an inordinately long time while the student looked for an academic reserve item for a patron. The trustee, while not angry, was a bit frustrated at the student's inability to simply ask the patron to wait just one moment while she opened the door. Later, I went through the scenario with the student who, only in hindsight, realized that attending to the trustee first, quickly, was probably the better decision. Problem-solving and decision-making skills go hand and hand, and they both, without a doubt, become more finely honed when someone can help the student with the reflection process.

### Be Judicious in the Giving of Praise

Unfortunately we live in a cultural climate where children have been raised to expect praise. Parents and teachers will often oblige with praise that is given profusely and indiscriminately. I can remember a specific time, very early on in my own work career, when I was showered with praise for performing a duty that was not only quite pedestrian but also one that I performed nearly every single day. The praise was condescending and embarrassed me. In fact, far from making me feel more confident and valued, I felt that I was somehow doing something very wrong indeed, and some misguided but well-meaning person praised me as a way of building me up. Students can see through insincerity almost immediately. When you do find situations in which a student is worthy of praise, make it count by being very specific. Instead of the slap on the back and the generic and well-worn "Good job," get specific: "Chelsea, I was ready to step in if you needed me, but you handled that angry graduate student beautifully. I thought there was not going to be a point where we could calm him down, but you managed to do just that by listening to his complaint and not raising your voice. When he claimed he returned the books, you gave him the benefit of the doubt by checking our shelves. When you didn't find them you asked him to look around his home one more time. That was a good call. Nice work." Specific praise targets the action and is a great way to help the students reflect on what they did that was so successful. Think about it: it would hardly help if you needed to correct someone's performance or behavior by saying, inscrutably, "Wow, you really need to improve." The student would be confused and would be well within his or her rights to demand: "Please tell me exactly what you mean!"

### Keep the Students Busy

At the circulation desk in my own library, this is a difficult thing to do. On any given shift, I have two students who sit in front of two OPAC computers and do any number of tasks, such as checking books in and out, answering the telephone, and so forth. I realize that some downtime at the circulation desk can provide a student with a needed breather when there is not, for instance, a full cart of books to be shelved or patrons checking out books. Often, though, I spend a good amount of time reminding students of what needs to be done, which is tiring. While this is not an ideal situation, it is part of the learning process. Eventually, if I have to continuously remind a student over and over again about something that should have been done automatically, but hasn't, I will shave a few hours off of his or her schedule. Well-placed consequences will help the student to make the connection.

### Encourage Ownership of a Task, Mastery of a Skill

In my own experience, nothing motivates more than being good at something. When students are allowed to excel at any given task and given the responsibility and ownership of a certain area in the library, they begin to self-motivate and develop positive feelings about their own abilities. This scenario has positive implications for other areas in their academic lives as well.

As professionals we can facilitate the development of motivation in our students by creating an environment in which their interest coupled with our guidance can take root, grow, and evolve. We need to encourage risks, tolerate mistakes, and reinforce each step in their progress no matter how small or insignificant it may seem, because all of these factors contribute to not only the growth of the student but also the smooth running of the library.

## Conclusion

Both working with students in the library setting and mentoring them along in their journey qualifies as a learning community, since students are learning and working with their peers with the guidance of professionals, though librarians may be reluctant to think of what they are doing in exactly that way. What better place than the library is there to inculcate motivation in our students? When we encounter students in the library who come to us with their research needs, or when we stand in front of a class giving bibliographic instruction, we do not question whether what we are participating in is, in fact, a learning community, because it simply is. While supervising students in the library does not directly parlay into formal mentoring, more often than not it does. Mentoring in the library, however informal it may be, is, for all intents and purposes, teaching, making the environment, the students, and all that it encompasses a veritable learning lab. We can model motivation to our students by showing an active interest in them, appreciating them, and helping them to understand how what they do, each shift they work in the library, contributes in a very big way. Hopefully, the sense of being depended upon to do a job well, being able to learn among one's peers in a supportive (and not competitive) environment, and receiving consistent positive reinforcement will keep the motivation muscle strong and well developed.

## RESOURCES

Borin, Jacqueline. "Training, Supervising and Evaluating Student Workers." *Journal of Library Administration* 21, no. 3/4 (1995): 87–93.

Davis, Barbara Gross. *Tools for Teaching*. San Francisco: Jossey-Bass, 1993. http://honolulu.hawaii .edu/intranet/committees/FacDevCom/guidebk/teachtip/motiv.htm.

Dembo, Myron H. "Understanding Motivations." In *Motivation and Learning Strategies for College Success: A Self-Management Approach*, 51–92. Mahwah, NJ: Lawrence Erlbaum, 2004.

Wolters, Christopher A. "Regulation of Motivation: Evaluating an Underemphasized Aspect of Self-Regulated Learning." *Educational Psychologist* 38, no. 4 (2003): 189–205.

# 10

# They Will Carry You Far

## Emphasizing Soft Skills

*Our work is the presentation of our capabilities.*
—Johann Wolfgang von Goethe

THOSE OF US who work with students in academia or in the academic library setting may see emphasis on "soft skills" as counterintuitive. Soft skills are perceived as not being as important as "information" or "knowledge" and are sometimes deliberately ignored when we are mentoring students because we believe that there are some things that can't be taught or shouldn't be taught. Instead, we learn to "accommodate" personalities, which can lead to the unfortunate labeling of students as "rude," "inconsiderate," or "self-centered." This creates a natural distrust on the part of the professional and can seriously impede any attempt toward a mentoring relationship with a student.

Accepting students for "who they are" and teaching and reinforcing soft skills are not mutually exclusive endeavors. In fact, all sectors of the workforce, from business to medicine (and everything in between), place a high premium on skills that engender ease and sincerity of communication with others. Since communication, in nearly every instance, is a key component in preventing misunderstandings and promoting good will, it behooves us as professionals to instill these skills in the students whom we work with on a daily basis. Ignoring these basic skills is to sacrifice a student's potential marketability later on, not to mention the opportunity for students to experience other successful interactions and relationships.

# What Are Soft Skills?

All soft skills can be said to be based one way or another on the way that we communicate with both ourselves and others. The implication for these skills in the workplace (and elsewhere) is self-evident. These skills include but are not limited to the following:

- To be able to listen and actually hear what another person is saying
- To be able to articulate one's own meaning in a clear and calm way
- To be able to demonstrate understanding of another's situation
- To be respectful of another's views and to gain respect for your own
- To be able to articulate your own goals
- To be able to negotiate through misunderstandings and conflict and come to a resolution that is satisfactory to both or all parties involved

# Can Soft Skills Be Taught?

Perhaps it would be fair to say that one cannot hope to teach soft skills in the same way that we teach other things, such as statistics, grammar, or biology. We do not, then, *teach* soft skills as much as we model them and reinforce them to our students. This will often mean that we will need to point out (always away from the sight and hearing of others) to the student when a student engages in unprofessional behavior in the workplace. If we are mentoring, no matter how informally, we are already having (or should be having) those types of conversations—teachable moments, corrections of misperceptions, and so on. Reinforcing soft skills involves isolating the explicit verbal exchange, going over it with the student, explaining why it was inappropriate, and then telling the student how to correct the response. There will be an explicit need for the student to be able to reflect on his or her words or actions, something that may be resisted. A certain amount of defensiveness can be expected, which can be exasperating to the librarian since it will be obvious that what transpired was clearly unacceptable. What needs to happen next is we must get the student to understand that it was unacceptable. Some student supervisors may think that these are skills that can be covered in student training sessions or by going over a list of customer service skills, but in fact they go beyond what a student needs to know for customer service. These skills take aim at the very heart of effective communication. These are life skills, and the perfect time to teach them is when our students are still in formation cognitively and socially.

## An Example

Here is an actual exchange between a nontraditional- and a traditional-aged student. The nontraditional-aged student (NT) is a graduate student.

> NT: I need to check out these books, but I don't have my student ID.
>
> T: Why don't you have your ID?
>
> NT: I work full-time and the Public Safety office is closed by the time I would be able to get here.
>
> T: Well, that's a problem.
>
> NT: Can you make an exception in my case? I really need these books!
>
> T: If I made an exception for you, I'd have to do it for everyone.
>
> NT: Can you suggest something then?
>
> T: Well, if I were you, I guess I would make time to get an ID. I feel like you are making this *my* problem and now *I'm* starting to feel harassed.

At this point, I stepped in, gently asking if there was something I could help with. I will often wait to see if the students can come to a successful resolution in such transactions. Many times they will and it is a gratifying thing to witness. Sometimes, low self-esteem and a sense of powerlessness in other areas of their lives will cause students to exert the little bit of "power" that they have sitting at the front desk over someone else. Fortunately, this is not something that happens very often.

The graduate student had turned red and was clearly upset. Understandably, she was unable to believe that the unpleasant interaction had turned into her being accused of harassing the student behind the desk.

I explained to the graduate student that my staff of students at the front desk were trained to enforce the one hard-and-fast rule that we have: everyone must have an ID for checkouts. I sincerely apologized for the misunderstanding between her and the student and assured her that I recognized her predicament.

She looked tired from hours of coursework after working an eight-hour day. I told her that I would be happy to make an exception and check out the books that she needed. I also offered to arrange an evening time for her with our Public Safety office so that she would be able to obtain her school ID, which she would need each time she checked out books.

She thanked me profusely.

All the while I was aware of the fact that my student was watching me.

"You caved," she said, looking angry and disappointed.

Because it was early evening, and I was getting ready to leave for the day, I told her that I wanted to talk to her about the incident the next morning. I did tell her that I felt the interaction was inappropriate and that she should think about how she handled things.

The following day when I had a conversation with my student, she felt confused at my reaction. "I followed the rules," she said. When I explained that it wasn't so much what she did as how she did it, I met with resistance. I asked her to think of a time when she felt that she was disrespected, particularly in an instance when she was given poor service or denied a service. She recounted a story of going to the local mall with her friends when she was in high school and wanting to get her ears pierced. The girls working in the piercing booth snickered at her and told her she needed a parent signature if she was under the age of eighteen. She told me that she understood the rule, but she felt ridiculed and belittled by the girls who worked there. I had typed up a transcript of the conversation between my student and the grad student, the same one that you just read, above. I asked her to read it and tell me where she might have begun to go wrong. Further, I asked her what she thought of the way I handled the situation. We spoke about a different way that interaction could have gone, one that would have been satisfactory for both parties: my student simply could have said, "Let me see what my supervisor says," rather than challenge and borderline bully another student. In my absence she could have called me or offered to put the books aside for the student.

## Reflection

As I have said, thankfully, I do not witness many such misunderstandings, but it is a vital part of the process to address them when they do occur. I did not expect my student to be thrilled about the fact that I stepped in on the exchange, overrode what she told the student, then confronted her about the exchange in a way that would force her to see her own mistakes, but in fact it was a teachable moment that I could not let pass. I worked consistently with that student at the front desk on what I liked to call her "various modes of communication," and I saw her make slow but steady progress. An important part of that process was to have her reflect back on problem interactions and find better ways of communicating acceptable resolutions. Confronting students at the moment when they exhibit rude or verbally aggressive or passive-aggressive behavior either among themselves or toward others will make them conscious of what they say and will train them to monitor and reflect on their own thinking processes.

## Strategies

- Model various soft skills at every opportunity.
- Discuss problems caused by the lack of soft skills.
- Confront students over rude or verbally aggressive or passive-aggressive behavior.
- Ask the student to engage in problem solving for a satisfactory resolution.
- Remind students to put themselves in another's shoes and to be aware of what the other person might be thinking and feeling.
- Have students recall a situation in which they felt they were treated unfairly or disrespected.
- Reframe the exchange using a successful style of communication.
- Encourage reflection on the situation and awareness of how they would handle a similar situation in the future.

**RESOURCES**

Georges, James C. "The Myth of Soft-Skills Training." *Training* 33, no. 1 (January 1996): 48–54.

Hughey, Kenneth F., and Judith K. Hughey. "Preparing Students for the Future: Making Career Development a Priority." *Journal of Career Development* 25, no. 3 (Spring 1999): 203–16.

Liptak, John J. "Using Emotional Intelligence to Help College Students Succeed in the Workplace." *Journal of Employment Counseling* 42, no. 4 (December 2005): 171–78.

Waggoner, Jacqueline. "Nothing Hard about Soft Skills in the College Classroom." Working paper, School of Education, University of Portland, 2010. http://mountainrise.wcu.edu/index.php/MtnRise/article/viewFile/67/49.

# When Things Derail (as They Sometimes Will)

*Experience is not what happens to you; it's what you do with what happens to you.*
—Aldous Huxley

*Fall seven times, stand up eight.*
—Japanese proverb

WORKING WITH STUDENTS in the library setting and mentoring them at the same time takes an incredible amount of physical and emotional energy, not to mention time and careful attention. Most students will be very appreciative of the time that you are willing to invest in them; however, the effort made by the professional on behalf of the student could suddenly take a wrong turn without warning. A student who may have begun to think of you as a "friend" will feel "betrayed" by the fact that one moment she seems to be learning valuable lessons at your knee and another moment she is being told that talking on her cell phone while at the circulation desk is inappropriate or that pajama bottoms and slippers, while certainly comfortable, are not proper work attire.

Because mentoring, in any shape or form, is relationship-building, it seems as though a certain amount of discord may arise as ideas or recommendations are rejected, offense is taken, or it is perceived that not enough credit or praise is given. Even the tone of your voice, on any given day, could send a student into a flurry of anxiety or disappointment. A student may ask "Are you mad at me?" or "Did I do something wrong?" This can be incredibly bewildering to the library professional and can, in fact, stop one in one's tracks.

Mentoring relationships with a student in the library can be complicated. This is in large part due to the less formal nature of the guidance you are offering students and specifically because you are their supervisor as well. In the library setting, the amount of mentoring being done will mostly occur in the times you encounter the student during his shifts in the library, though if the relationship turns out to be particularly successful, the student may further seek your counsel separate from that which he will receive while working his hours in the library.

It is difficult, if not impossible, to keep the kind of distance that might prevent any chance of discord or misunderstanding. Moreover, if, indeed, the library professional keeps a student at a distance, what kind of "mentoring" relationship will really be able to take hold? Because most library professionals will not encounter the students who work for them as their students in the classroom, they may be perceived in a different way than faculty, even if, professionally, they are faculty.

Unfortunately, the specter of dysfunction is alive and well anywhere relationships may form.

## Specific Problems That May Arise

If a problem should arise with a student you are mentoring, it could have a detrimental effect on other students who are observing the difficulties or who have heard about them from the student herself. It is important (and perhaps obvious) to note that dysfunction may be perceived on the part of both the student and the professional at any given time.[1]

*Some Reasons Why Things May Go Wrong*
- A student may fear a poor performance appraisal.
- There is jealousy of you or other students that develops into mistrust.
- The student feels that he or she has no "input" into the relationship.
- The student is unable to separate his or her actual job responsibilities from other aspects of the mentoring process. For instance, the student may find comfort from developing a friendship with the supervisor or may begin to see him or her as a kind and wise parental figure.
- The student may feel as if his or her goals are not being achieved.
- The student may begin to have disregard for the job if he cannot see what he is explicitly contributing.
- The student perceives the professional to lack any real empathy for his or her actual situation, whether it is financial, emotional, or academic.

Dysfunction in the mentoring relationship may present itself in a number of ways:

- Passive-aggressive behavior
- Sarcasm
- Physical aggression toward the professional or others
- Bewilderment
- Sadness
- Hopelessness
- Emotional outbursts
- Harassment
- Clinging

With the lists of what could go wrong and the reactions that follow, the realization may set in that whatever we call the relationship that we have with a student, be it friendship, coaching, mentoring, or guidance, requires, to say the least, a delicate balance. Fortunately, things more often go right than they go wrong. However, the professional must be vigilant of her own behavior. The impression that you have on a student working in the library affects her on many levels and is one that she will tend to take to heart.

## A Cautionary Tale

I once employed a student whom I quickly perceived to be a godsend to both the library and myself. She was a very self-possessed student, intelligent, full of wit, enthusiastic, well-spoken, and hard-working. I couldn't believe how lucky I was that because her off-campus job didn't work out, she would be working with me in the library. While her academic major was sociology, she quickly developed a keen interest in all aspects of the library and librarianship. It was like a whole new world had opened up for her. This kind of keen interest in how things function in our setting most certainly is not the norm, and so I was surprised, to be sure, but incredibly delighted. She gently peppered me with questions on each of her shifts and expressed a desire to have further responsibility. After a short period of time, I gladly gave her specific responsibilities.

Soon, she was functioning in a student supervisory position and was seemingly handling her academic workload with aplomb. I would often look at her and think, if I had half of that drive when I was in college, I would have saved my parents an untold amount of grief, not to mention myself. Life could have been so much easier!

We moved through the summer semester and my student arrived, on time, every day, ready to tackle any number of projects. The library would not be horribly busy until the fall semester began; my student began to submit ideas to me about organizing academic reserves, relocating our leisure book collection, and other ambitious projects. I squirmed just a little, because while the library itself was not that busy, the summer is the time we librarians do our research and any number of various things that the normal semester does not allow time to commit to. I knew that the projects she mentioned would require heavy input from me. I compromised and prioritized, choosing just a few. She seemed mildly disappointed, but didn't say much. I felt glad that I could set limits while at the same time give her the opportunity to accomplish something she seemed eager to do. After all, so many of her ideas were good ones.

While she kept herself busy, I noticed other members of my student staff getting quiet around me, or I would find them congregated when I would come from my office out to the circulation desk. They'd disperse, ignoring the student who was helping to supervise their activities during the day. My student gradually changed her communication style with me, which went from one of slightly respectful deference to bold statements about, among other things, "handling" students who don't seem to "know their place" at the circulation desk. *Red flag.* And then the red flags turned into huge red banners waving in the ferocious winds before the impending storm. And what a storm it was. Maybe some of you reading this will have seen it coming. Maybe some of you would not have had a clue. I probably could have spotted a potential problem quicker if it was a student working closely with one of my colleagues. You can all guess correctly that it was a downward spiral from the point of that first red flag. But in reality, the trouble started long before my perception of it. Then the unrelenting questions that dogged me for quite some time: Why didn't I see it? Was I that obtuse? What had I done wrong? Who was more at fault—me or my student?

## Taking Responsibility

The professional must take responsibility, period. This does not mean that the student, in any way, is always blameless. It simply means that in a relationship in which there is an unequal balance of power, the person with the "power" is responsible for doing the least amount of harm disengaging themselves and the student from the relationship structure.

Self-reflection and reflection on the sequence of events will surely help to frame the experience and help prevent a repeat occurrence in the future. The sense of betrayal can be intense, for both the student and the professional. The rupture of the relationship, even a dysfunctional one, can cause very real pain.

From the student's point of view, I believe she had begun to feel as though I was her most trusted friend, her ally, a "me and you against the world" type of scenario. I had been unaware of the fact that despite her many and varied accomplishments, she was not well-integrated socially on campus. I felt bad for her in that respect and tried to pair her with other students in the library on projects, which never seemed to work out. I had, quite honestly, thought nothing of the fact that she called herself an "old soul" and was thus aligning herself with someone of my age and experience. When she began waxing rhapsodic about librarianship (think of the last time you encountered a student who thought library school was a *great* idea), an abrupt shift from her passion for the field of sociology, I thought it was an initial excitement that would fade away once she became entrenched in the job. Of course I was wrong.

There is an old adage I once heard that states relationships usually end in exactly the way they begin. There is some truth to this as it can apply to any relationship, though it perfectly described my relationship with this student. Making the connection with someone willing and eager to learn can be a heady experience in the academic setting, where many of us, most especially librarians, continuously meet students at the same developmental levels. The connection I describe was a swift one at its inception and, unfortunately, it ended the same way.

## By Any Other Name

I did not call myself the student's mentor. I did not call myself her friend, her coach, or her guru or guide. In fact, I didn't have to. The nature of working with students in the library setting is that often such a relationship will evolve whether we are cognizant of it or not. As I stated before, so much of the so-called mentoring that we do will come about spontaneously, often in an unstructured way, without a label. This is a satisfying situation to find oneself in—to be able to meet students where they are developmentally and work with them in the setting in which they have been placed. We are mentors, in fact, when we are not really even fully aware of it. But in fact we must be alert to the perceptions students may have and all the more so because we are functioning as their supervisors as well.

## The Aftermath

My experience was a lesson learned. The situation felt like a failure to me all the way around, as I failed to perceive, early on, how far my student was straying from her initial interests, something I could have mediated more frequently and early on. I felt that I let my student down as well as myself. I experienced an extremely brief but intense period where I wondered if all of the effort involved in mentoring a student, albeit even in an informal way, was really worth it, especially if a situation that looked and felt so promising at the outset could fail so spectacularly.

In reality, problems are unavoidable, unless we are automatons without the capacity to think or feel.

The student and I parted ways, but the situation was not without severe bitterness, anger, and disappointment on her part. I know that I was left with some emotional scars and more than a few misgivings. It caused me to reflect, deeply, on all that had come to pass. I can only hope that, given some time to reflect, the student was able to learn something from the experience. It seems inevitable, though, that she, too, suffered in ways as well. I heard that she had swung right back into her major, sociology, having left her interest in librarianship as quickly as she had taken it up in the first place.

## Strategies

- Don't rush the mentoring relationship. Instead, allow things to unfold. It takes time to know someone, and the work environment adds another layer of complexity to this.
- Build rapport and a communication style. Being open and approachable will build trust over time.
- Provide some sort of framework for the mentoring process, however informal. Consider an "open door" policy where you make yourself

available to students. Schedule regular meetings or make it a point to have regular casual chats.

- Goals keep things process-oriented but keep the end in sight. Finding out what a student is interested in will help to pinpoint the exact job in the library that is most suitable for him or her.
- Acknowledge progress. This cannot be overstated. Students rely on evaluation as a way of both motivating themselves and gauging their own progress.
- Communication should go both ways. Elicit conversations with the students, which will allow for the venting of frustrations, fears, doubts, or satisfaction.
- Be fair. Try to imagine how uncomfortable and unprofessional it would be if your boss played favorites. Understand how a student feels.
- Remember that the student's primary function in college is her class work: for example, your goals are not her goals. Acknowledge that while her position in the library serves a vital function, school is her first priority. Work with her on balancing both.
- Address concerns when you see them. The habit of gently correcting behaviors when you see them will help a student to see that such feedback is normal in the workplace and does not always require a "sit down" conversation and that such feedback will help them.
- Refer students to campus resources if necessary. For instance, a student who may seem inordinately angry, sad, or homesick may benefit from an appointment with the campus counselor, an impartial and trained professional who is in the best position to help the student develop coping strategies and who will also be able to ascertain whether or not the student is developing a problem that goes deeper than what is seen on the surface.

## Conclusion

There will be situations in which we begin an informal mentoring process with a student and not be able to see the implications for dysfunction early on, but that may be because we are not looking for them. While it may seem counterproductive, at best, to begin any kind of relationship with the thoughts of what could possibly go wrong, mentoring students, even in the informal way that is most likely in the academic library setting, one must be aware of any rents in the fabric early on. In my own experience, they do not just appear out of nowhere; be assured that the signs will be there if you look for them.

When I look back on the relationship that I have just described, I see possible problems presented themselves early on, though I may not have been willing to see them. Perhaps you, as the reader, did too. It seems clear in this particular situation that I got well ahead of myself and felt too much enthusiasm over having a student whom I identified with so much because she reminded me of myself at that age: eager to please and possessing a near limitless desire to learn all that could be learned.

Proceeding slowly, ascertaining a student's possible goals and interests, and knowing both your own limitations and those of the informal mentoring process will help to both contextualize and frame how you will proceed with the student. The librarian cannot prepare for every eventuality—relationships, by their very nature, are unpredictable and things may not always go the way we'd like them to. But optimistic caution on our part can help to mitigate the factors that can cause a downward spiral.

## NOTE

1. Terri A. Scandure, "Dysfunctional Mentoring Relationships and Outcomes," *Journal of Management* 24, no. 3 (1998): 449–67.

# 12

# When All Is Said and Done

*Every new beginning comes from some other beginning's end.*
—Seneca

*You cannot hope to build a better world without improving the individuals. To that end each of us must work for his own improvement and at the same time share a general responsibility for all humanity, our particular duty being to aid those to whom we think we can be most useful.*
—Marie Curie

*The habit of looking to the future and thinking that the whole meaning of the present lies in what it will bring forth is a pernicious one. There can be no value in the whole unless there is value in the parts.*
—Bertrand Russell, *Conquest of Happiness*

IT TURNS OUT, as these things usually do, that writing a book about mentoring was not as straightforward as I would have hoped! The literature abounds with theories and definitions about the practice, as approaches are formulated, studied, argued about, assessed, dismissed, and reformulated. Mentoring occurs in nearly every sector of business, medicine, education, and so on. The models used are often complicated ones, built on more fixed power structures and discipline-specific. My dilemma, then, became how to clearly differentiate between my strategies that blend the librarian/supervisor's role with that of a third role, the mentor. While I used many of the basic principles of mentoring and looked to the experts, I combined those with my own experience and my own strategies. One caveat is that there is no "one size fits all" strategy and that most of us who attempt a mentoring relationship with someone will find what works for both them and their student.

The debate never seems to end about the impact librarians have on educations. We are seen as primarily "trainers" rather than educators and are not seen as mentors, per se. The larger academic community may not think of us as mentors, though our positioning in working with students in our libraries affords us golden opportunities to help navigate students both academically as well as developmentally in the workplace.

Mentorship, of any kind, no matter how formal or informal, is a commitment, plain and simple. It requires both time and commitment and can alternately be exhilarating and exhausting. Most of us will embark on mentoring of the informal kind. This is a process that takes time to find a communication style, a framework, and a context—yes, even informal mentoring requires some elements of these aspects!

Each encounter is bound, by the infinite variety of personalities and needs, to be different. I have literally lost count (yes, I used to keep track of these things!) of the number of different scenarios presented to me over the years, though I have valuable insight from them. I have learned, too, that not every student will be open to the experience—some may be hard to "reach" or connect with for reasons that will forever remain unknown to us. Some students will seek us out because they are readers and they like to be around books and they know that we do, too. They will connect with us because we are science fiction fans, or we love popular culture, or Jane Austen, or gaming. There is often a spark, but not always. A reluctant or shy student may come around. The one who was enthusiastic, initially, winds down and retreats. Several of my mentoring relationships involved students who had no interest in being involved in anything of the sort. As one student told me, when I engaged her in conversation about her years at the library at lunch one day (a year after graduation), "I had chosen a school away from home to get away from everyone who was always in my business—I really just wanted to keep to myself at school. I wanted to finally grow up." Eventually, my interactions with the student eventually turned into an informal mentoring relationship, though I intuited how she felt initially. I would engage her in small talk which she did not resist, but was careful never to add anything else that would keep the conversation going. She was a good worker and things seemed quite fine the way they were.

She is now married and successful, though hoping to move further along in her field. Despite the mild "push-back" she exhibited, eventually I gained her trust. The well-worn dictum "slow and steady wins the race" is best exemplified in this case. Relationships take time. "Progress" happens (when it does) in small, sometimes indiscernible increments and is not always easily apparent. We work, the student works, and we give guidance, engage in conversations, make suggestions, listen to bouts of despair, and all along the way lessons are being learned and ways of being, both in the workplace and in the world, are being formed.

Reflecting, over time, helps the librarian to process his or her own feelings about specific and strategic conversations, setbacks, suggestions made but not followed, and, of course, the triumphs along the way. And while we cannot compel the students we mentor to keep a journal, recording the same types of things I have mentioned, it does not hurt to suggest it to those who we think may be so inclined. Frequent conversations with our students in which we employ our active listening skills will help them to hear what they are saying, evaluate, and then reflect.

## Assessing the Outcomes

But how to measure the results of our efforts? Librarians and educators love assessment; in fact, to a great extent, our work depends upon it. We live in a results-driven world where progress must be seen immediately in order to justify any number of factors. It is difficult, however, to assess the relationship-building we engage in with our students. In fact, part of the beauty of informal mentoring in the academic library setting is the fact that the process is relatively free of all of the usual measures put in place that anticipate and require results, missing the incremental and important changes and milestones along the way. This is not to say that assessment has no place in the mentoring process; in fact, I believe there be should some assessment, however informal— just much less so for the purposes that I have set forth in this book. Perhaps the best kind of assessment might be librarians gathering together to discuss their experiences with their students and how they limn the line between supervising them in their work-study jobs and guiding them toward their own goals. The dual roles, though, are not mutually exclusive. We are often doing both without really realizing it. Exchanging strategies and experiences can be an incredibly helpful process and can buoy the librarian who encounters problems anywhere along the line.

## Only Engage

Wrapping up the mentoring process with a student who is leaving your employment because of graduation, transfer, or any other reason can be emotional. Bonds that are often made are not necessarily broken, but are definitely "interrupted" and changed. We may continue to mentor the student from afar, but we cannot deny that the relationship will change, in fact has already changed, since proximity is no longer an option. Putting formal closure on an informal relationship only seems paradoxical, but it isn't. Reflecting on specific aspects of the student's time at the library, along with encouragement and praise if these are warranted, will go a long way. What did they like best? Least? What had they become proficient in that they had no clue about previously? What are they still struggling with? I am fascinated when engaging in these types of conversations to hear a student's own perceptions of herself from one point in time to another and feel gratified when I can see that intellectual and emotional growth has taken place. Even more gratifying is when the student herself is cognizant of her own transformation.

I have found that the mentoring I have done with students has benefited me in ways I had never expected it would. My students have taught me to have more patience and to be more tolerant. They have often elevated our conversations to places I never thought they could go, thinking deeply, analyzing, and scrutinizing while they figured things out. In this way the mentoring relationship comes to be an exchange of sorts and, in my opinion, a fantastic experience. I have learned that I do not always have to be the sage, the wise guide, the all-powerful role model who knows everything and can solve all problems. Some days I can't remember where I left my coffee cup! I am able to tell a student, occasionally and with honesty, "I don't know." The mentoring relationship, at its very core, should be an honest one.

Finally, we will not be able to reach every student. That is just a simple fact. But for those we can and do reach, we should keep our minds and hearts open to what the possibilities may be. The student you begin with will not be the person you end with. Time, indeed, does its work on us all. In the end, everyone changes. And thankfully, with the help we give along the way, it is almost always for the better.

## RESOURCE

Mullen, Ellen J. "Framing the Mentoring Relationship as an Information Exchange." *Human Resource Management Review* 4, no. 3 (Fall 1994): 257–81.

# What a Difference Four Years Makes!; or, The Inevitable Disengagement

*All motion is cyclic. It circulates to the limits of its possibilities and then returns to its starting point.*
—Robert Collier

*Tomorrow, and tomorrow, and tomorrow / Creeps in this petty pace from day to day.*
—William Shakespeare

ONE INTERESTING ASPECT of working with students is that we often see them all at the same developmental level. Roughly, most freshmen we meet will be at the same level, as will sophomores and so on. This is a perfectly normal and expected situation, of course, though I am certain that many, if not all of us, would love the opportunity to see real, identifiable growth in the students who work with us. This is not always possible for a variety of reasons, including the high turnover that many libraries see in student employment.

Sometimes, though, we are able to hold on to a student who begins work at the library as a freshman and stays for his four years. Because the goal is always to somehow, on some level, mentor, however informally, every student who comes to work for us, we could be nurturing an important relationship in the beginning though not even be aware of it.

I have had the luck and opportunity to have had students work with me for all four years of their college career, and I marvel at the many aspects of their development that have taken place right before my eyes, though so incrementally that I am not even aware of it as it is happening, though of course it does.

## It Is Not Always a Straight Line

I once had the opportunity to work with a student whom I perceived, correctly, as amazingly well-rounded. She inquired about a job at the library, telling me how much she loved books and was a hard worker. She had a gleam in her eye and gave a small squeal when I asked her to come back the next day for an interview. She showed up early. When I met with her I quickly determined that she had not been awarded work-study, but I assured her if that situation should change she should come and see me. About a week later, she came back to the library, had pleaded her case, and was awarded work-study. I was incredibly impressed and a little taken aback by her assiduous attempts to make herself eligible for the library.

During her freshman year she learned vast amounts and performed each and every duty assigned impeccably. During her four years with me, her level of dedication, amazingly, never wavered, and I dreaded the day when I would lose her to graduation, as I do with so many good students, but she'd been with me for four years.

Then it happened. The dreaded "it" can be almost anything, but in this case "it" was a loosening or breaking-away process that it seemed, developmentally, this student needed. And looking back, it was probably inevitable for her to go through in order to disengage herself from a job that she had not only fought for, but performed well in, and had loved.

About six weeks before graduation I began to see changes in my student, which I put down to her pressures over her thesis, a project she worked doggedly on, but whose exact focus had changed a few times, causing her a lot of anxiety and displeasing her academic advisor. I understood, and I told her so. She'd sigh. I assured her that it would get done—that everyone who graduated lived through the writing of a thesis. She would smile and say "thanks," but I noticed, then, that a shift had clearly taken place.

I stepped back, realizing that something was happening that neither of us could control. Although it was difficult not to jump in and try to make things "better," I watched and waited.

She'd grown increasingly quieter on her shifts at the circulation desk and was irritable when I would have to remind her to do her shelf reading or any other number of work duties she'd performed on her own without my ever having to ask her to do them previously.

One day, I gathered about six of the students working that morning and handed out tasks for each of them to complete. My student looked at her slip of paper and simply lost it, right there.

"You're kidding, right?" she said, looking straight at me, her face flushed red with anger.

I am ashamed to say I was too stunned to reply at first, and I stood there, with my mouth gaping.

The other students watched to see how I would handle the situation, no doubt taking careful note as to what was possibly "negotiable" in the assignments I had just given out.

"No, I'm not kidding," I finally managed to say. "We talked about this a few weeks ago," I continued, attempting to keep my voice even.

An outburst on my student's part ensued.

I asked the other students to carry on with the jobs I had assigned them, conflict being a terrible spectator sport. My once stellar student and I were now at what seemed like a standoff. I felt confused and incredibly uncomfortable. I had never expected this.

She'd had a book in her hand that she slammed down onto the circulation desk. She turned around and walked through the glass doors of the building, mumbling something under her breath. I called out to her, but with her back to me, she raised her hand above her head, angrily and dismissively waving me off.

I looked at the one remaining student manning the circulation desk and asked her to tell my student, when (and if) she returned, that I needed to speak with her in my office. I felt my face flush.

I sat back down at my desk and felt my heart beating fast. I'd never, once, had trouble with the student. Even more, I'd never had a hint, in any way, that she could have been capable of such blatant disrespect. But now, she had openly disrespected me, her boss, in front of other students. In addition she had left the building in a huff, without my permission, while she was on her shift.

There had been nothing overt that would have precipitated her outburst. At least that's what I had thought, at the time.

## We'd Come So Far

Stop and think for a moment how any of you reading this scenario, right now, might react.

What would you do next?

Back in my office, I will admit that I felt not only dismayed but also angry. My immediate thoughts were that she had just tossed away four years of a wonderful mentoring relationship and that she was ungrateful for all that I'd done for her. But immediate thoughts are not best thoughts, and I forgave myself for my initial, though natural, reaction to the situation.

Or was she?

When she came back to my office, I could see that she'd been crying. But I could also see that she was still angry. I did not have to prod her. She sat down across from me and just cried. Out came some weak excuses for her behavior along with a few minor grievances she'd been harboring. I listened without interrupting, though I will admit that it was not an easy thing to do. I thought that it was important for her to be able to lay her cards on the table. However, after a bit, when she took a breath, I had a few words to say, myself.

## All Is Not Lost

I started with the immediate issue at hand. I addressed her behavior that day, period. I asked her to think about how things had gone down that morning and asked her to think about what might have precipitated the episode. She began to visibly calm down when she realized that I was not going to berate her, yell, or otherwise accuse her of anything, but instead I stayed strictly focused on what had just happened.

"I have so much on my mind," she continued. She told me that the career plans she'd been nurturing (in which library school had been under careful consideration) had suddenly met with disapproval from her parents. Finally, she said, in a quiet voice, "I'll miss this place." Then she said, very quietly, "Hey, I'm sorry. I really am."

I told her that I understood. And at that moment, I did. I really did.

My student was moving through the difficult disengagement process. We'd had a close and fruitful mentoring relationship that was coming to a fast end, and that fact, coupled with the dashed hopes of the career she had in mind for herself, had come to a head.

## A Decision to Make

It became very clear to me what I needed to do. With a mere three weeks left in the semester, I decided that it was time for my student's exit. I aimed to make the process as painless as possible, but it had to happen.

Anyone might think that given the student's wonderful history with her work-study job in the library, just about anything short of murder could be forgiven, especially given the fact that she would graduate in just a few weeks' time, but that wasn't the way that I saw it.

I felt that the outburst happened for a reason. I would never have chosen to have her job end in the way that it did, but in retrospect I am not sure I or anyone else for that matter could have prevented it. Developmentally in her own process, it seems as though her outburst was almost necessary for her to segue into the next phase, whatever that phase might be, and disengage from an environment that she had "grown up" and into. Nothing lasts forever, even though we'd like it to.

## Saying Goodbye

Remember being cruel to be kind? Well, sometimes it is necessary. I did not miss the opportunity to mentor her, even as I was breaking it to her that it was time to move on. I asked her to reflect on what had happened and how a scenario like that might play out in a job in the "real world." I could see the misgiving in her face as her impulsive action began to slowly dawn on her. We hugged and I told her I looked forward to seeing her at graduation in a few weeks. I told her she had a lot on her plate between now and then and that she'd be thankful for the extra time. She just needed to focus.

## The Sendoff

It was a defining moment to see her take her diploma on a gorgeous spring day. She was jubilant. I marveled, not for the first time, at how fast the years fly and how that fact will become painfully apparent to my student, in fact, all of my students, almost immediately after graduation, when time is no longer measured in the increments of semesters but instead five days of work for that coveted weekend.

My student did not get to library school (not yet, anyway), but an opportunity presented itself and she went off to teach English overseas, providing her the chance to fulfill another dream she'd long harbored: to travel the world.

I am in frequent contact with this student and listen with great pride and satisfaction as she tells me of her adventures abroad and both her personal and professional accomplishments.

Only once had we spoken about "the incident," both of us recognizing it for the aberration that it was. It was not something that I would have allowed to end or shut down the relationship. It was important, though, to send just the right message, both to her and to the other students who watched both fascinated and appalled. I made the decision I thought best and gave the student a graceful out, thus ensuring that the integrity of our relationship, at least in the short term, was not compromised.

The relationship had clearly changed, as it was destined to do.

# The Mentor Learns Something

Mentoring literature is rife with cautionary tales about how mentoring relationships can end in less than desirable ways. I have read many of them, dubious as to why a mentor would allow a situation to get so out of hand. Then I "woke up" and realized that because of the fact that human relationships can only be "negotiated" and people cannot be "handled," anything can happen.

Looking back, I should have checked in a bit more with my student, perhaps "relieved" her of a few of her shifts, thus lifting some pressure off of her shoulders. Ultimately, I should have begun the process of "disengagement" much earlier than I did. This could have been done by "winding down" the duties of my student, asking her for her expertise in training some of her peers working with her at the circulation desk, effectively "handing off" all of the responsibilities she'd performed so effectively during her time at the library. I could have engaged her in more conversations about endings, in general, but commencements, as well: that while our relationship and the cozy confines of a situation in which she felt both valuable and capable was ending, it was all in preparation for something wonderful—the next step.

# A Success Story

Most endings will not be nearly as emotionally charged as the one that I have just recounted for you, nor as dramatic. Most students, in my experience, are ready to move on to the next phase of things. You will have seen them exhibit signs of "senioritis" that seem to coincide with the warmer weather and thoughts of packing up and going home. Those last few weeks and months can bring a mixed bag of emotions, but ones that most students will handle with grace.

Nina worked at the circulation desk from the time she was a freshman. On "moving-in day," her father, a soft-spoken man, approached the circulation desk and asked about potential jobs on campus for freshman students. I always welcome the opportunity to speak with the parents of new students because I like to tout our beautiful campus and our wonderful philosophy of learning. It is also an opportunity to put their minds' at ease when they find themselves in the position of being separated from their child for the first time.

Nina hung back a bit behind her father. I informed him about job opportunities on campus that were available to students who were awarded work-study in their financial aid packages. During this time, my future student never said a word, though she stood listening to the conversation with a smile on her face. He asked if there were any jobs at the library his daughter might be able to apply for. I addressed the girl with huge brown eyes and asked her if she was interested. She replied that she was. I could see that her father was ready right then and there to seal the deal, but I shook his hand, telling him how lovely it was to meet him and both welcomed his daughter and wished her luck.

"What about the job?" he asked me. I told him if Nina was still interested in a job after she'd moved and settled in on campus, she should come and see me. While a parent myself, I appreciated her father's concern that his daughter have employment, and while I fully understood his imperative to take those initial steps for her, I didn't think it sent a good message to the student. After all, students are going to live on their own, so they might as well start taking the initiatives for their new lives on their own. I also never expected that the student would come back to the library, since her father failed to secure the job for her. I assumed they would move on to another office or department on campus.

A few days later, Nina came to see me at the library with a very spare but neat résumé she'd assembled. I interviewed her and made sure that she thoroughly understood the job description and what would be expected of her. I judged her to be just a bit immature, perhaps from being sheltered, but pleasant and eager to please. I hired her. She initially chose late night hours, calling herself a night owl, but her parents nixed that, not pleased that during her first semester she would be working late into the night when she could be sleeping. I bristled a bit, but still, I understood. I've often thought many times since how lucky I was that her parents felt the way that they did about her late hours; otherwise I would not have had the opportunity to get to know the interesting person she was nor have the honor and opportunity to mentor her, though neither of us, initially, would have categorized the pleasant interactions we were having at the circulation desk as a mentoring relationship. Because she was dependable I came to rely on her to guide the other students along regarding customer service and the other many and varied details behind the desk. She became a student whom other students looked up to. The shy girl I met on moving-in day proved to be a perfectionist, a student who had an intense and burning desire to get her teaching degree, please her parents who supported her unconditionally, and perhaps forge a life beyond the small coal mining town where she grew up, knowing the lack of opportunity there.

Here is a situation in which the casual and informal mentoring that librarians have the capacity to provide in the library setting is exemplified at its very best. Over the four years that I watched Nina mature and change in various ways, I tried to guide her, ever so gently. I supported her educational goals, provided opportunities for extra hours, thus extra money, wrote recommendation letters, listened patiently when she suffered through a very intense and all-consuming relationship, struggled in its aftermath, and triumphantly found her level footing all over again.

We had no confrontations, though in all fairness, neither of us was ever the sort, though there could have been because students often have very intense emotions that are not always easily hidden or controlled. I always tried to "meet her where she was" no matter what so that I could understand at all times where she was coming from. While she never missed a shift, she was rather transparent and I knew when things were not going so well with her. I'd sit with her at the desk and engage her in light conversation and, eventually, whatever was on her mind would come spilling out. I am careful never to ask questions that are too probing or personal, though I will listen to what a student wants to tell me. And I have learned that the quickest way to have a student clam up in the middle of a conversation would be to act shocked at something they have shared with you.

During Nina's last semester, she asked to have her schedule adjusted since she needed to travel to different elementary schools to do classroom observations. Afterwards, she'd come to work in her professional clothes and a more self-possessed way about her. She became quieter, as she seemed to be homing in on wrapping things up at the place she had called home for the past four years. I realized it for what it was: a winding down of our mentoring relationship, which seemed to happen as organically and naturally as it had begun. This was actually initiated by Nina herself before I ever instigated a shift in things. As I have said before, this is actually what all mentoring relationships lead up to, the step that is called "disengagement" in the professional literature on mentoring.

Because my mentoring relationship with Nina was steady from the day that it first began (though this may not be true for all mentoring relationships, no matter how formal or informal) the disengagement process, while tinged with sadness, was inevitable. Nina actually needed (whether she understood this consciously or not) to begin the process of pulling away and begin the process of thinking about her life beyond the confines of college, because real growth had taken place.

### Full Circle

Graduation day is a bittersweet one for me. I usually graduate quite a few seniors, and even though I may not have had close mentoring relationships with all of them, it is poignant to see them go, not all of them fully ready for the next step.

The day of graduation I had some flowers for Nina and a bottle of wine for her parents, who I'd seen here and there through the years when they'd come to campus to visit their daughter. I'd grown incredibly fond of them. When they came into the library that morning, we embraced and cried, while they expressed immense gratitude for my "looking out" for their daughter for all four years. They told me they could not adequately express the comfort it gave them to know that someone cared about her that much and had helped her out in so many ways. I felt emotional, though embarrassed, at their words of praise. Positioned as I am and working with so many students, it would seem a dereliction of duty, in so many ways, not to take the opportunity to mentor students. Our very existence in the academic setting is because our students exist. They matter and they are well worth our efforts.

### Relationship Redux

I wish I could say that my and Nina's relationship continued with regular telephone chats and drop-in visits. It hasn't, but I had not really expected that it would, despite my desire. Nina is a busy elementary school teacher with a busy social life. She is happy and well adjusted. Every once in a while I receive an e-mail from her updating me on whatever is going on in her life at the moment and occasionally I will drop her a line, as well, telling her funny stories about my new crop of students at the circulation desk and whatever else has changed about her old job. The relationship that was, is no longer. It has not ended per se, though it has changed. This would be the "redefinition" stage of the mentoring process and, like the disengagement stage, is inevitable. People change and grow, as they should.

## Strategies

David Clutterback and Gill Lane, in their wonderful book *The Situational Mentor: An International Review of Competences and Capabilities in Mentoring*, detail action steps for the mentor that can aid in the successful ending or transitioning of the mentoring relationship.

- Prepare the mentee for the fact that endings can and probably will occur as the relationship fulfills its purpose.

- Recognize when a relationship is maturing.
- Review the relationship regularly.

Further, they suggest that the mentor should possess the following skills if the relationship should need to be acted upon and "shut down":

- Assist the mentee to accept and embrace the ending process.
- Develop a clear and mutual understanding of what has been achieved and how the relationship should evolve.
- Make the ending point clear.[1]

## Conclusion

Mentoring relationships, most especially regarding the informal kind we are more likely to have in the library setting, will always be in a process of "ending," much in the same way that from the day we are born we are in the process of dying. Our students are just that—students, primarily, and not library employees. It can be said with a large amount of truth that just as they begin the job, the end is clearly in sight. It is inevitable and is a fact that they often understand better than we do.

As librarians, we can vow to be as "present" as possible in all of our dealings with our students, which can help us to avoid the mistake of making our contact with them mere "do this" and "do that" transactions, which can easily happen given our many duties and time constraints, further compounding the problem of missing opportunities to shepherd the relationship carefully. And while it is common knowledge that endings are inevitable, they don't have to be approached with dread and foreboding. In fact, quite the opposite—preparing for them, along the way, in increments, will provide a wonderful springboard for students, in which they look to the next step with expectation, armed with, hopefully, more self-confidence and knowledge about themselves and the way the world works than they began with.

### NOTE

1. David Clutterback and Gill Lane, *The Situational Mentor: An International Review of Competences and Capabilities in Mentoring*, Gower Developments in Business Series (Burlington, VT: Gower, 2004).

# Afterword: One Student's Experience

**Erin E. Bruno**

THOSE WHO HAVE graduated in the past few years with a degree in journalism or English know how difficult it can be to succeed in today's job market. Competition has grown fierce as more journalists find themselves downsized and emerging technologies crush the old world of print media. I first faced these challenges head-on in 2008 when I found myself downsized from my first job out of college as an associate editor on a promising medical publication. Three years later, I still cannot erase the bitter, cold January memory—walking out of the office for the last time with a box containing my personal belongings, blindsided and shocked, having no idea where to turn. Never in a million years did I believe that even with a college degree, impressive portfolio, and diligent work ethic I could be let go from a job. Unfortunately for me and thousands of other young college graduates, I launched the beginning years of my career in an economically unstable and technologically advancing environment that frowned upon the print world. The shock of losing my job continued during the subsequent months and morphed into a bitter disillusionment as I found it increasingly difficult, if not impossible, to find another job in my field.

It was a fierce determination and almost absurdly positive attitude, along with competitive networking skills and a keen ability to adapt to a changing environment, that helped me persevere and succeed during this trying time. I first gained these character traits and professional skills working as a circulation desk student assistant at Arcadia University's Landman Library in the fall of 2005.

After transferring to Arcadia University from a community college in northern New Jersey, I was a stranger at this private liberal arts college just outside of Philadelphia. During my first day of work, Michelle Reale welcomed me with her warm, inviting personality and affable yet gentle attitude. Michelle taught every work-study student who walked through the library's glass doors how to embody a positive, professional attitude by her own example. By offering both formal and informal lessons as well as copious and frequent feedback and conversations, Michelle invested her time in us, focusing on our strengths and working to strengthen our weaknesses.

Michelle encouraged the best in her students, never abandoning her positive, nurturing attitude. I witnessed this firsthand during my last semester at college. At that time I experienced a difficult, depressing period while trying to balance the demands of life with school and work; disheartened and overwhelmed, I began calling out of work. After the third day, I remember Michelle calling me, sternly insisting that if I did not show up to work the next morning we would need to part ways, but then adding, "If you need anything or need to talk, I am here." The next morning, reluctantly, I returned to work, and from then until graduation I did not miss a single day at the library. Michelle's "tough love" taught me the importance of, among other things, "showing up." This perseverance in the face of both uncertainty and adversity helped me when I lost my job in 2008.

While one can maintain a positive attitude and stay determined, perhaps even more essential to success in life is the ability to adapt to a changing environment, which I learned quickly when I started my job at the library. Although the job seemed fairly uncomplicated, like handling matters with students, faculty, and visitors, soon it proved challenging to me. At times it could be anything from an argumentative student denying a book was late or a demanding professor insisting on booking a room for a class although it was already occupied. Sometimes it would mean that I would have to deal with an issue by myself during an early or late shift. In such situations, I learned as much from watching my mentor as I did from the instruction she gave me directly. Now I realize that I was learning from her even when I didn't realize that I was!

In the past couple of years, while looking for a full-time job in my field, I have worked several temporary and part-time jobs in many different industries and fields, including medicine, corporate housing, finance, and banking.

In each industry and field, I have used the skills that were nurtured in me at the library—skills I did not initially possess, but learned, such as how to act professional, how to deal with difficult people and situations, and how to be in the work world.

As well as character traits, I gained several essential professional skills while working at Landman Library, networking among them. While working in the library, students would communicate among themselves about internships, job prospects, and opportunities on campus. Michelle always encouraged her students to network with one another and with other students and faculty we encountered on campus. Often, she would make introductions or set up opportunities for us to meet other professionals who might be able to help us. Michelle herself introduced me to the *Wild River Review*, an online literary publication, where I eventually interned during my last year at Arcadia. These networking skills that Michelle encourages and that I first discovered at the library became vital for success in my career.

The inspiration and life lessons gained from a trusted mentor can make all the difference in who we are and what we can become. We learn valuable lessons from our mentors, if we are lucky enough to have them, lessons that can guide us from one stage of our lives to the next. Michelle was mentoring me from the first day I set foot in the library. It all unfolded in a very organic, informal way. Still, I feel immense gratitude for the variety of lessons that I learned at the elbow of someone who truly cared and in fact still does care.

# Index